FORGIVENESS
WITH
MEHER BABA

This is writing to be savoured; to be reflected upon and to be reread. Laurent and his companions have given us something that is deeply profound and transformational – perhaps not immediately but certainly as with anything of truth a gradual realisation of how we can better our lives and those of others. The authors are guided by the life and words of Meher Baba but even if you are not a lover of Baba's you will gain an immense amount from the ideas and application of forgiveness in your own life.

R.G. Lewis (England)

Ultimately, there is no-one and no-thing that we do not have to forgive, if we are sincerely "homeward bound." My teacher Yogi Bhajan taught that our karmas are something that we must become reconciled with, or they will never be transcended. He taught that there are five very important things that we must forgive in order to do this:

1. Forgive God that He separated you from Himself and created you as a creature.
2. Forgive your destiny that it is as it is.
3. Forgive the distance and the environment which are always challenging and the cause and effect which are happening.
4. Forgive your capacity, your ability, your duality and your divinity. Please forgive it, it is limited.
5. Forgive yourself that you have to go through it.

Haring Singh Khalsa (Arizona)

With the guidance of this book, I was able to forgive some people that I had never been able to with any other method. For several months I was stuck in anger and resentment even after doing a ton of forgiveness work. But when I found these techniques in *"Forgiveness with Meher Baba"*, they gave me room to allow those angry feelings as valid, but then to find the linchpin that was holding them in place and finally, truly forgive and let it all go! Thank you, thank you, Laurent & friends for leading me to freedom and delight now. It's sooooo beautiful to turn my "enemies" into "just fellow humans."

Jane

I find this book to be a shining gem. It is written in an unusual style. The words spacious and inclusive spring to mind. It has a simplicity and a subtle, loving power that is challenging, inspiring and reassuring. To me, it does not present as a didactic book written by an 'expert.' It is more a sharing, an offering from a fellow traveler and companions who have valuable experience, insights and ideas. It is an invitation to be receptive, and to actively participate. It is a practical book, facilitating, if one is open and ready for it, a deep inner processing. It calls upon me to clarify, to face where it is that I am holding to lack of forgiveness, be it towards others or towards myself and to feel how that impacts my energy, my daily life. It provides a framework in which to explore and to allow the unravelling of the 'knots' of thought and emotion that bind and inhibit my capacity to forgive thereby restricting the flow of love.

Bronnie

Published by OmPoint Press
Wilmington NC

ISBN 978-0-692-72257-2
All rights reserved.
©2016 by Laurent Weichberger

First Edition May 2016
Second Edition December 2016
Third Edition January 2017
Fourth Edition October 3 2018

Contributing authors hold copyright to their chapters.

Cover design Ed Legum
Book design Karl Moeller

Printed in the USA by IngramSpark

Front cover photograph: Avatar Meher Baba on March 15, 1937 at Meherabad, India. Photographed by Rano Gayley.
Courtesy www.msicollection.zenfolio.com
and © 2016 Meher Baba MSI Photographic Collection,
used by permission.
Thank you to Christine and Martin Cook.

FORGIVENESS

WITH
MEHER BABA

LAURENT WEICHBERGER & COMPANIONS

OMPOINT PRESS

TABLE OF CONTENTS

Another Word by Rick Chapman
Preface by Aspen Weichberger
Introduction by Vanessa & Laurent Weichberger

PART I: BY LAURENT WEICHBERGER

TABLE OF CONTENTS

PART II: CONTRIBUTING AUTHORS

"Laurent's book will transform lives.

Laurent shows what is needed on Earth to break these violences and we need this in the world of today.

This Life-cycle diagram he created should be used in the schools or in conflict resolution programs in university.

Good job, Laurent."

JEAN PAUL SAMPUTU

Ambassador of Peace
Interreligious and International
Federation for World Peace

On the anniversary of Sept. 11,
Jean-Paul Samputu sent out this message.

From: Jean Paul Samputu
Date: Tue, 11 Sep 2018, 4:25 p.m.

"You can't be common. You have to be willing to do what others won't do, to make sacrifices that they won't make, to go the extra mile, to take the high road when others take the easy way out, to forgive when it's not fair, to resist the temptation when others are giving in. There's nothing you're facing that's too much for you to handle. For every struggle, every temptation, every difficulty, God has given you the grace to stand strong. You have the power to be uncommon."

Another Word

Forgive me, in advance, for adding yet one more voice to the chorus of excellent voices represented in this book, voices that tackle the issue of forgiveness as it pertains both to our mental and emotional health as well as to our spiritual well-being. Forgive me, I say, because in all honesty I don't believe that the book requires another voice: Laurent is compelling in his conversation with Vanessa about the origins of his preoccupation with the subject, and his daughter, Aspen, speaks with uncommon eloquence and perception in her own introductory remarks; and the individual accounts speak quite personally and adequately for themselves.

But Laurent has asked me for a brief comment about this new and expanded Fourth Edition of his book on forgiveness, and so I offer this: there is really only one reason to forgive anyone for anything, and that is the same reason that we must eventually forgive everyone for everything: as Avatar Meher Baba has definitively stated, each one is none other than God Himself, the very Divine Beloved of all beloveds, and He alone plays His Game of Creation—plays all the parts, ours included—all to realize, one soul at a time, that He alone exists and that there is and has ever and always been nothing whatsoever to forgive.

Rick Chapman
October, 2018

A Prayer

Beloved God (Allah, Parvardigar, Paramatma) hear our prayer that our sin of making two from the Oneness of Truth, be forgiven and forgotten in the rediscovery of the unity of all religions and faiths in our search for our nature of Infinite Oneness within Your Being.

Most especially we ask for your Grace to erase the causes of the strife and bloodshed in which we have all participated thus far into the manifestation of Your infinite Divine consciousness which we repeatedly neglect in our delusion of furthering Your Truth by such acts.

We ask for forgiveness and forgetfulness in the Truth of the Oneness of all in which we are endlessly joined into the Truth of Your Being.

Beloved God, I promise that if it is your will to answer my prayer, I will do my utmost to live my promise to you on this day to remember and practice the glory of Oneness.

Don Stevens

Preface

Forgiveness with Meher Baba was written for several reasons.

First, throughout the forgiveness seminars done by Laurent and others, there were many common issues being addressed. He felt that he learned so much through facilitating the forgiveness seminars that was never captured in *The Doorbell of Forgiveness* or other texts. Laurent wanted to take the information, and the seminal discussions of the seminars and make it available on an individual basis, without compromising the anonymity of those who shared their experiences. While doing the forgiveness workshops as a group can be beneficial, it isn't required for the techniques presented in these chapters to be effective. Laurent also felt that Don Stevens wished for him to continue his forgiveness work, and delve deeper into the mechanics of forgiveness.

Secondly, Laurent and other members of the community wished to provide a reference and a medium in which to share the thoughts and processes that many have found successful in their own personal journeys. Each of the individuals who contributed to, or are mentioned in, these chapters have had personal or professional experience with these issues. Finally, he wanted to work to make the content of the forgiveness seminars more accessible to a wider audience. Some struggled with the style of the previous book, *The Doorbell of Forgiveness* – so this volume is also intended to present the material in a clear, concise, and easily consumable style.

My own experiences, as the editor of this book, have been somewhat unexpected. My attitude towards therapy and self-help has been referred to as "Good Will Hunting" in style. (Just that I don't like therapy but I found the book to be useful.) However, I found the contents of the chapters triggered a deep self-reflection and analysis of my own forgiveness processes. I found that just by absorbing the information and learning about others' journeys it aided my own awareness and process of forgiveness in my life. Some of the styles presented did not really align with my own processes or emotions – but others I found extraordinarily helpful, something that I believe varies greatly depending on the person.

I do believe there is something for everyone here and I hope the reader is as pleasantly surprised as I was.

Aspen Weichberger
March 9, 2016
Myrtle Beach, South Carolina

AVATAR MEHER BABA
at Upper Meherabad (India) in the corridor near the East Room,
15 March, 1937. Baba had come on a day trip to Meherabad.
Photographed by Rano Gayley.

Introduction

By Vanessa and Laurent Weichberger

VANESSA: How did Don E. Stevens come to focus on forgiveness in his life?

LAURENT: The first time I ever heard Don speak about forgiveness was in London, not long after I had moved to Sussex, England in 2003 to work with him on what would become his authorized biography. I would make frequent visits to his London flat, where we would work for a day or two (or sometimes three) on various spiritual projects for Meher Baba. He called it going about his father's business.

It was during one of those visits that he explained to me directly about an editorial he had read by William Pfaff in the International Herald Tribune, his favorite newspaper. The author was suggesting that the best way forward for the two sides engaged in a decades-long bloody conflict was for See *The Doorbell of Forgiveness* (London: Companion Books, 2011), p. 20. them to simply completely forgive each other, and move on peacefully. Pfaff's suggestion had a profound impact on Don, as he wrote:

> "Pfaff's insight that only forgiveness can free the karmic racial entanglements of the Balkans is a very great truth." [1]

I have been asked, why this suggestion from Pfaff had such an impact on Don. While I can't be certain, I do remember having discussions with Don about this, and the impression I got was that Pfaff was making a giant leap, such as scientists speak about when discussing Einstein's theories. In other words, instead of trying to tackle the deep wounds of the Balkan problem, with political and other types of worldly solutions, the suggestion to directly apply forgiveness and move on was simply incredible to Don. I think he agreed with Pfaff in a radical way, that forgiveness had that much power to dissolve seemingly impossible tangled knots, in a practical way.

From that day forward he tried to integrate forgiveness more and more into his own life, or as he would say: "in my own backyard." One result was that he started to envision Meher Baba's work with the different faiths; Baba characterized this repeatedly as bringing the world faiths together, "Like Beads on One String." Don felt Baba's work was directly related to forgiveness. In fact, beyond envisioning this forgiveness work, Don would receive "intuitive" guidance on this subject, which took the form of lengthy writing sessions over many years. We captured many of Don's intuitions on forgiveness in *The Doorbell of Forgiveness*, so I won't reprint them here. However, I should quote from one that I reference frequently, so that you can get the gist of what he was saying. On September 14, 2007 in Paris, Don wrote an intuition which he titled, "Forgiveness 3" as follows:

Forgiveness is the ultimate test of the ego. To condemn is the ultimate declaration of separateness. In this incarnation I have reserved for my true devotees the expression of complete forgiveness, first in their own lives, and then in the teaching to others of the example that they are qualified to make for others. Do not confuse my function in this lifetime with the activity I have included importantly in other lifetimes when my lovers have built religions around my words. As I told the press in London on my first visit in the 30s, I have not come to establish a new religion in this lifetime, but to revivify the world's existing great religions and gather them together like beads on one string. [2]

Of course, when reading such an intuition it is immediately clear that the voice Don writes with is not his own. The voice references Meher Baba's visit to London in 1931-1932. During that time Don was 12 years old living with his family in California, with his mother, step-father and two brothers. Also the use of words like incarnation would only make sense from the voice of Meher Baba, as Don would never speak about himself this way. I brought these issues up with Don, and he admitted that from time to time in his intuitive work he knew the voice he heard within was that of Meher Baba, but he was reluctant to admit this. He warned people against thinking that what they hear within was directly from God. He wanted people to "true" their intuitions. This all may sound contradictory to some, and I understand that, but I wanted to be honest in saying that Don was extremely careful about ever

See *Meher Baba's Gift of Intuition* (London: Companion Books) for more about truing.

saying, "Baba told me..." and wanted Baba lovers to be careful about that habit as well. I think that is at least in part where the motivation for "Truing" came from.

The intuition "Forgiveness 3" continues, but the main point being made was that the numerous travels Meher Baba made throughout his life wherein he personally visited, and repeatedly bowed his head at, worldwide spiritual centers and spots associated with the greatest mystics of the past, was directly related to helping humanity with this work of forgiving one another. Don felt this was especially true when it came to forgiving hatreds fueled by religious differences. Of course, the total number of locations is too numerous to comprehensively list here, but to name a few off the top of my head, we know Baba did spiritual work at:

1. The Zoroastrian Fire Temple at Udvada in Gujarat, India, which remains one of the holiest sites for Zoroastrian pilgrimage, containing living fire brought by the Zoroastrians from Persia to India. [3]

2. Various Hindu sites, including the Shiva temple at the Ellora Caves, in Maharashtra, India. Baba also visited the places associated with Sadguru Ramakrishna of Calcutta, India more than once with his Mandali.

August 12, 1924 they visited Ramakrishna's place Dakshineshwar for the first time. (See Lord Meher p. 544).

3. The Dilwara Temples, the primary place of pilgrimage for the Jain faith.

4. Sarnath, India, a place of pilgrimage for the Buddhist tradition, where Buddha preached his first sermon at the Deer Park.

5. Many Christian places, such as those associated with St. Francis of Assisi, in Italy, as well as St. Theresa of Avila in Spain. He visited the cathedral at St. Mark's in Venice, Italy, and when in Egypt he found and visited a cave used by Mary, Joseph and the child Jesus in Egypt on their flight from King Herod.

    This cave was at the bottom of a Coptic church, where Baba visited August 1932. See *Lord Meher* p. 1466.

6. Many Sufi locations, such as the tomb of Qutub Moinuddin Chishti in Ajmer, India, and the tomb of Imam Reza in Persia.

    Starting June 6, 1931 Baba visited Reza's tomb three nights in a row doing special work there. See *Lord Meher* p. 1225.

There are many other locations, but this is a good sample. Again, Don felt intuitively, as we read in "Forgiveness 3," that by Baba personally working spiritually in these and many other locations, he was laying the groundwork for humanity at large to deeply forgive one another in a way that has never been done before.

VANESSA: What was Don's story of forgiveness?

LAURENT: I remember one story Don told us, which while he didn't use the word forgiveness when he told it, does shed light on what Don's experience was of Baba's forgiveness. This takes place during the late 1950s or early 1960s at Meherazad, India.

So there was a singing program arranged, whereby the Baba-lover singers from Ahmednagar wanted to come to Baba's home at Meherazad to sing for Beloved Baba in Mandali Hall. Baba explained this to the men Mandali, including Don who was visiting Baba at the time, and told them not to be late for the program.

Meher Baba started to shift his work from Meherabad to Meherazad at the end of 1943. See *Lord Meher* p. 2391.

Later that day, Eruch and Don decided to take a walk together down the little dirt road that leads from Meherazad to the main road, one of Eruch's favorite walks. While they were walking away from Meherazad, they saw the truck with the Baba lovers from Ahmednagar headed towards Meherazad with all the singers and instruments. As the truck passed them going towards Baba, Eruch said, "We are sunk. Oh well, let's finish our walk." So they went a little further, then turned and headed back walking to Baba at Mandali Hall. By Don's watch they were still before the start time of the program, yet Eruch's words had him quite nervous. When they finally walked into Mandali Hall and the Baba lovers were setting up for the program, Baba was sitting in his chair, obviously looking around for Eruch and Don. At this point Don was afraid, and literally stood behind Eruch, trying to hide. Baba started with Eruch and gave him a tongue lashing about not being in the hall with Baba before the singers arrived, and all that. Then, looking around Eruch, Baba, with lightning flashing in his eyes, pointed his

See: *Meher Baba's Word and His Three Bridges* for Don's version of this story.

finger right at Don with the words, "And you, Don – you have ruined my day!" At this, Don said he completely "disintegrated." Of course he did not literally disintegrate but he said the force of Baba's gesture and words was so profound that everything stopped and he came apart, and then, just as suddenly he came back together and was aware of everything again and heard Baba's words, "Never mind, forget it, let's have fun." And with that, the clouds parted, and the storm subsided, and he noted that something had happened to him. The way he explained it, something was gone that was there before he was disintegrated by Baba. I am not sure that either Baba or Don ever used the word forgiveness but that is the story I remember.

I have been asked, "Why is this the story I remember from Don's life with Baba, and what do I feel is the significance?" Those are good questions. Well, to start there are many elements of this story. Baba told them when to be back for the program, Eruch saw the truck pass them, and instead of running after the truck – he decided to enjoy the rest of the walk, even knowing that they were going to catch hell from Baba when they returned. Don hiding behind Eruch when they returned. Baba telling Don, "And you ruined my day." It is all so dramatic, and Baba did not immediately forgive, but really let Don have it between the eyes. The fact that Don felt that Baba's upset somehow disintegrated something within him to me was the height of the drama. Then it all came back together with a light hearted – never mind ... let's have fun. It all sounds so Baba! I guess the significance to me is that there are times to forgive, and times to not forgive, and it all works out in the end. Don's feeling that Baba was really upset with him shifted something. Once that shifted, Baba also shifted. It is like a game, and maybe the significance for me is knowing how and when to forgive, and to remember this is all a game. I know in my own life, when I am really struggling, with my son Cyprus, or something like that, and feeling like I can't let go – that story comes up in my consciousness, and I just suddenly say – forget it, let's have fun. Not always, but when I can remember and let go, I try to do it, and the results are great.

VANESSA: Do you know of Don's personal stories of forgiving others?

LAURENT: There are only two stories that I can remember which Don told me about forgiving others in his own life. And I will try to explain them as best I can since they are somewhat complex.

Don only attended one year at Black Mountain before transferring to Johns Hopkins University where he became a Chemistry major.

The first story he spoke about in his books, *Some Results*, and *Sexuality on the Spiritual Path*, and it concerns his first homosexual experience with "Mac." The relationship was troubled with that individual, and Don was actively trying to work through his issues with Mac who had gone away traveling at that time. This took place while Don was a freshman student at Black Mountain College in North Carolina.

Don told me that his attempt to write to Mac about his struggles and apparently forgive him were thwarted by Mac's sudden and untimely death. Don found out about Mac's demise by the letter he wrote to Mac being returned to him unreceived and unopened. While Don never expressly told me about his forgiveness process with Mac, as it was intensely personal, I could tell that Don was working hard to resolve something within. With Don's inability to communicate with Mac, it was my observation that Don found other ways to work through those early traumatic feelings. Now, looking back on all that, and reflecting on my own forgiveness challenges, it is clear that the forgiveness process requires great patience.

I have been asked about my personal reflections and insight on this story from Don's life. I would offer this, that Don was trying to work through his issues directly with Mac, but couldn't because Mac died. Because of this, he had to work through these issues in a more indirect way. This necessarily included multiple relationships, wherein he could get closer to the heart of the issues he needed to resolve, but also required greater patience on Don's part. See: *Some Results*, chapter on Mac, for more about this story.

The second story took place decades later in France, where Don worked with Claude Longuet on real estate projects. There was a particular man renting one of their properties who was named Balbeur. This fellow was being somewhat difficult and apparently was also suffering from diabetes. Don wrote about this in an email to me that contained his intuitions about the forgiveness work he did with that man. The intuitive voice speaks clearly to Don:

> Your own repeated experiences of falsity and extreme expression of personal ego on the part of even those chosen by Baba to be in his company must similarly be balanced and redeemed finally by your own acts of complete and

spontaneous forgiveness. It is only in this manner that you can truly be a true part of your beloved Baba's work. This is the counterpart of unconditional love. It was what you gave Balbeur within an instant, and which he recognized within the instant... You gave true forgiveness, although ultimately it was an illogical act... You must be prepared for such illogical acts of forgiveness in your participation in your Father's life. [4]

VANESSA: Can you explain about Don's development of forgiveness workshops and their intent?

LAURENT: Yes. The first time we had a workshop on forgiveness with Don was the weekend Young People's Group (YPG) seminar during October 20-21, 2007. This was the seventh seminar, each previous one having its own theme. Don had sent us the theme of forgiveness about a month prior to the gathering in California, and we had our homework. We were told to reflect on the meaning of forgiveness and to bring something to share about that. Danny Sanders and I rode the train from Flagstaff, Arizona together for that adventure, and I wrote my homework on the train.

In any case, we did share about forgiveness that weekend, and Don said a number of things to us about forgiveness which I will repeat here as high points. For the entire conversation you can read all of Don's sharing in *The Doorbell of Forgiveness* as that has just about everything he ever said about it.

Don told us at the YPG seminar: "The most important spiritual work in the world today is that of forgiveness." He was extremely certain of this. I think it is relevant to note that Meher

Baba during 1966 said that the most important spiritual work in the world was to get young people to desist from using drugs. Baba told Mik and Ursula Hamilton, "Go to America and dissuade young people from taking drugs. Encourage, persuade them to stop taking drugs! To do that is the highest spiritual work to be done in the world today." See *Lord Meher*, p. 5218. See also the book: *A Mirage Will Never Quench Your Thirst.*

During the seminar we were encouraged by Don to look at all the ways forgiveness could transform the world, from extremely personal examples between two or more people in an altercation of some kind, up to national levels, such as Israel and Palestine. All in all, Don was convinced that the New Humanity as Baba spoke about it had some serious forgiveness work to do, and we had no doubts about where Don stood on this by the end of the weekend together. I for one was deeply inspired to undertake this work.

Don urged us at that same seminar, just before it ended, to make a personal project of forgiveness, "in our own backyard." He said only when we can forgive in our own lives will we be authorized to speak about forgiveness to others, and he wanted us to speak about forgiveness to others, but to live it first. He wanted us to select a person (or situation) and work on it after the seminar. I chose to forgive my father for his suicide, and I did (it took some time), and then I wrote about my process in the book *The Doorbell of Forgiveness*. Don loved that chapter, and subsequently asked me to share more about forgiveness with others.

The last time I saw Don was in Los Angeles in 2010. We had gone together to an extremely aggressive meeting where the local Baba lovers were trying to resolve a series of conflicts that had arisen at their center. We sat together with one of the key parties in the conflict to lend her our love and support. Afterwards, having witnessed the hatred and anger expressed at this Baba group meeting, I wept in my seat. I was deeply troubled and sad. When we returned to the home where we had been staying, Don took my hands and said, "Little Bear, I want you to return to that group and do forgiveness work with them." Don passed away less than a year later.

After I recovered from Don's passing, I wrote to that Baba group, and told them what Don had asked me to do. I ended up preparing the first Forgiveness with Meher Baba seminar for that group, and have performed it twelve times (as of this writing) with various groups since then. While Don never directly developed any of the forgiveness seminar content with me, nor did he ever explain to me his intent, I intuitively grasped what he intended, and I started by using the book *The Doorbell of Forgiveness* (which we had just created together) as my guide.

VANESSA: What was Don's definition of forgiveness?

LAURENT: In *The Doorbell of Forgiveness* I published everything I could locate that Don had written about forgiveness, and it was quite a bit of material. While Don was not big on "defining" things, he certainly spent a lot of time and energy trying to understand the "mechanics" as he would say, of the thing he was focused on. After all, Don was trained as a chemist, and he was a scientist for sure, as well as a great mystic. When I was contemplating this, I picked up *The Doorbell of Forgiveness* and found a passage from Don that works well to describe his feelings about this, even if they fall short of an actual definition:

Forgiveness for me falls instinctively into the domain of love and unity. It would be difficult to try to pair two more imposing keys to God and Creation than to put these two words side by side. After all, if infinite indivisible unity is a fundamental characteristic of God, and if we reflect that Baba has said very clearly that love is the high road of all roads to Realization, then it is evident that one has mated two horses that are almost bound to win the course. [5]

However, I am certain Don would not want me to leave it there. Since Meher Baba asked Don to create a book with him, which became *Listen, Humanity*, based on Meher Baba's life and words, I will quote Baba from *Listen, Humanity* about forgiveness:

I can forgive; I have come to forgive. Forgiveness is the highest thing for those who are forgiven. It is not a great thing to me to forgive. In fact, in reality there is nothing to be forgiven, for there is really nothing like good and bad. You find them so, and they are there in duality, due to your own bindings in duality.

In the bondage of duality there is good and there is bad, but in reality everything but God is zero. Maya, which causes you to mistake illusion for reality, is present for you but not for me. For me, only I am, and nothing else exists.

It therefore means nothing for me to forgive, and everything for you to be forgiven. [6]

VANESSA: What were Don's wishes for the forgiveness workshops?

LAURENT: To be completely honest, Don passed away before we ever had even one conversation about forgiveness workshops. At that time, I was just totally focused on completing *The Doorbell of Forgiveness* for publication, and wanted Don to have a copy of the book before he passed away, but unfortunately he passed in April 2011, just three months before we printed the book. I have felt guided by Baba and Don regarding the Forgiveness with Meher Baba seminars, so much so that I wanted to write this book as a reflection of all that I have gathered from performing the seminars with so many lovely Baba lovers around America.

My darling daughter, Aspen, encouraged me to share this as part of my introduction to this book, so here it is:

Is My Forgiveness Wholehearted?

In my own life and forgiveness work, I have found the single most important criteria is to ask myself, am I wholehearted about forgiving? I seem to be allergic to the notion of forgiving: "because you should." I don't know why, but for some reason, unless I am wholehearted about my decision to forgive I feel I am still – in process. I forgive myself for not being ready to forgive another. In the case of my forgiving my father for his suicide, it took me over twenty years to wholeheartedly forgive him, and then I felt it was accomplished naturally.

Aspen responded to this by sharing with me, "Many think forgiveness is just a choice and then it is over. Addressing the time necessary is important, and it is okay for it to take time."

This highlights the difference between forgiveness as a verb – the process of forgiving, and as a noun – forgiveness, that which is "given" as the result of the process. I think this process is actually different for each person given their outlook on life (their "nature"), the way they were raised ("nurture"), and even their past lives ("sanskaras" or impressions). Maybe some feel that they should forgive, and don't need to be wholehearted, so that is not a barrier to forgiveness. In any case I do recommend that one not force the issue, and perhaps there are some natural phases, and other emotions to process before jumping straight into forgiveness. We address this in the section on "A Sample Forgiveness Life-Cycle" later in this book.

[1] From an email to Laurent, December 8, 2004, Subject: "Whew!", Ibid TDoF p. 197.

[2] *The Doorbell Of Forgiveness*, p. 201. (Hereafter TDoF)

[3] See: https://en.wikipedia.org/wiki/Udvada (accessed Dec. 25, 2015).

[4] *TDoF*, p. 197.

[5] Ibid, p. 192.

[6] In *Listen, Humanity*, by Meher Baba, (edited by Don E. Stevens), p. 68, as found in LH.pdf.

Chapter One
What is Forgiveness?

IN ALL THE SEMINARS WE CONDUCTED over a few years, the same initial questions arose from the participants, such as, "What is forgiveness, anyway?" In other words, the word forgiveness seems to be very little understood, and beyond the shallow phrase, "Forgive and forget," there seemed to be extremely little to work with. Let us understand the word more deeply, and see if we can arrive at some conclusions.

When attempting to define forgiveness, it is important to realize that we are defining both the meaning of the verb, actively forgiving, as well as the noun (what is given or received with forgiveness). This definition may actually be both personal and contextual depending on the giver, the receiver, and the situation that is being forgiven. Maybe the ultimate definition is left to those involved, and their story will explain it better.

So, I researched the verb to forgive (and the noun forgiveness), and was fascinated to see it defined as a type of giving up, as in the choice to pardon, or more literally to "give away" one's right to punish another, when entitled to do so based on the circumstances:

Verb, forgive:[7]

    : to give up resentment of or claim to requital for <forgive an insult>

    : to grant relief from payment of <forgive a debt>

    : pardon <forgive one's enemies>

    : to stop feeling anger toward or about (someone who has done something wrong)

    : to stop blaming (someone)

    : to forgive someone for (something wrong)

Noun, forgiveness:

    : the act of forgiving someone or something

    : the attitude of someone who is willing to forgive other people

If one gives up or gives away one's right to punish someone who has done "wrong," then this type of a spiritual gift is rare indeed. We will explore the meaning of this gift, and many of the ways forgiveness may be given as well as received.

Another important point was made by Charles Haynes, at the Meherana Spring Sahavas (May 2014). When I asked if he could share his feelings about the importance of forgiveness, Charles responded:

Yes. Forgiveness is the key to freedom. Without forgiveness, one cannot be free to live the life of love and service that Baba would have us live. Forgiveness, of course, is not the same as reconciliation. Forgiveness can – and should – be done internally within one's heart. Reconciliation requires that both sides come together and acknowledge what needs to be forgiven. Those who feel they have done nothing that calls for forgiveness are not easily reconciled.[8]

Charles implies that forgiveness may be limited in what it can achieve, or that you can reach reconciliation without forgiveness but then again perhaps forgiveness transcends the need for reconciliation. Perhaps then, to forgive someone you must also surrender the wish for true reconciliation (which process may bog down interminably).

Further still, there are considerations regarding who has to be involved for forgiveness to be effective and complete. When I first brought up this question with Don Stevens and his Young People's Group there was an immediate division in the group. Some people felt that both individuals, the forgiver and the forgiven, must be present and actively working together, while others were certain that forgiveness could be accomplished individually, without the other party even being aware that forgiveness work was being done.

See *The Doorbell of Forgiveness*

Since we are still in definition mode, why not define what doing something wrong means? Many people call these actions that require forgiveness bad or evil. However, in the context of forgiveness with Meher Baba, we will shy away from such harsh judgments, and prefer instead to think of these as mistakes of judgment, errors, or actions that were not the best or highest choices. The reason we are going in this direction has to do with the non-dual approach of Baba, wherein he helps us to understand there are really just degrees of good, and what we call

3

evil is the least amount of good. He says people act out in ignorance, and eventually all are destined for the divine goal of Self-
realization, or God-realization, which knows no limitations.
This understanding is helpful in our forgiveness journey.

Of the errors, I feel it is important to remember that there are
two basic types: errors of commission and errors of omission,
the latter being much harder to see. I remember when I explained errors of omission to my daughter Aspen about ten
years ago (when she was around eleven years old), she just held
her face in her hands. It was as if she had just been told the most
awful thing: that she could have been making mistakes all along,
about what she should have done, but did not do. Oh well, live
and learn, right?

Aspen recently shared with me,

> I remember for me one of the hardest parts of this realization
> was how much people (and myself) – don't do – out of fear,
> and the courage required for action, and that you can harm
> someone so much because you were simply too scared to
> act.[9]

This brings us to the notion of what I like to call the "Forgiveness Directions," or – in which direction is the forgiveness
moving? This is what we will discuss fully in the next chapter.

---

[7] Definitions provided by merriam-webster.com

[8] See OmPoint International Circular #14, p. 15 at
http://www.ompoint.com/OmPoint_Circular_14.pdf

[9] From Aspen, June 30, 2015.

Chapter Two
Who Actually Forgives?

> The weak can never forgive.
> Forgiveness is the attribute of the strong.
> — MAHATMA GANDHI [10]

WHEN WE FIRST STARTED DOING FORGIVENESS seminars in 2012, I was inspired to consider the forgiveness directions (as in compass directions). Over time, and twelve seminars later, the list has evolved into these categories, although I am sure more will emerge. I give an example of each for clarity:

FORGIVING ONE'S SELF

After reflection and contemplation, it is clear that one has done something wrong, or made a mistake, or error, and some lesson was thereby learned. In order to keep moving with a healthy and happy positive attitude in life, self-forgiveness may be required. It means to stop punishing oneself for the mistake. This seems to be related to a sense of repentance and remorse for some action, and a quote from Meher Baba comes to mind:

> With justification there is no hope for repentance, and without repentance there is no hope for change. [11]

FORGIVING ANOTHER PERSON

While this may seem straightforward, sometimes it is not. Complexities arise even after a few moments of contemplation, such as:

~Have we clearly identified what the other person did that requires forgiveness?

~Is what we have identified as the "problem" needing forgiveness actually a very large and complex issue, which can be broken down into smaller issues? In other words, is it possible that it is so complex that different aspects of the issue can be forgiven at different periods of time? Instead of trying to tackle the whole issue at once, can it be done in pieces? This was certainly the case with my second major forgiveness project in my own life. I forgave some aspects of it immediately, some later, and I am still working on forgiving other aspects of it. That may sound strange, but it is honestly how I am dealing with the issues. When I looked at the whole situation it was overwhelmingly painful, so I started to break it into pieces and forgive the pieces.

~Do we need the other person to ask for forgiveness before we are willing to give our forgiveness? This can actually be a huge hurdle for some people.

~Do we perhaps feel that person needs to acknowledge that they did something wrong – before – we feel we can forgive them? In other words, do we have any criteria in mind, before we feel another is actually eligible for our forgiveness?

～What if that other person is not reachable, not interested in communication, or perhaps already dead – what then?

～What if you know that forgiveness is ultimately needed but you have so many other emotions and feelings swirling and erupting that you just can't forgive – right now – wholeheartedly? Aspen shared with me, "I feel too that sometimes allowing yourself the time to feel those emotions and grieve or be angry – or whatever the case may be – is actually a healthy part of the forgiveness process. That forgiveness means feeling those things, and processing them and moving beyond them in a constructive manner." [12]

～What if the person you are trying to forgive did something to someone else, not even to you directly? Aspen shared with me, "It is easier to forgive harm to yourself and much more difficult to forgive harm to those you love." This is something I was just contemplating, and it is a total confirmation of how I also feel. If someone harms a loved one, close to me, it is much harder for me to forgive. I want to punish them, and it takes a great deal of effort and self-control not to do so. This brings up a new notion I have of what I will tentatively call a "forgiveness triangle," discussed in the chapter, "Towards a Forgiveness Geometry."

In a perfect world, you are able to forgive the person for their mistake, however an important point here is that it may also mean that you decide that your relationship with that person needs to shift in some way. Forgiveness may mean that there is still love, but that the structure of the relationship needs to change. An example of this from my own life is that I had a giant "Aha!" moment, when contemplating deeply my second major forgiveness project in my own life. In the second project, I had to come to terms with forgiving an individual that was very much in my present daily life. At the time I was completely torn, because I saw only two options: forgive them and forget it, and resume my relationship with them. Or, don't forgive them and leave the relationship once and for all. That seemed like an impossible situation at the time, until I was shown that I can in fact forgive the individual and leave the relationship. In other words, forgiveness was shown to me as not meaning that I had to keep the relationship "as it was" because it is up to me how I wish to relate to that individual after forgiving. When I realized this, it was like being let out of some mental prison. I ultimately did just that, I forgave (and still am working on forgiving some parts of the situation), and I moved on from that relationship. So while the individual is still in my life, the relationship bears no resemblance to what it once was. This is a truly liberating experience for me.

FORGIVENESS PUBLICLY AND ON A GLOBAL SCALE

The President of the United States, for example, is allowed to give a "Presidential Pardon" which can be used to dismiss any punishment pending for an individual who has been found guilty of breaking a law in America. However as Aspen shared with me, "Presidential pardons are usually political moves, rare at best and mostly forced. There is almost never sincerity or emotion behind it..."[13] This raises the question then, does an act of forgiveness need to have "emotion behind it" or be deeply felt to be considered real, or effective? How can anyone judge the sincerity of another's act of forgiveness? It reminds me of Meher Baba saying not to judge the quality of our own love for God, or him. In other words, loving is more important than the quality of love. Or it is better to practice loving (and deepening the quality of love by practice) than it is to wait for some future where love is more pure. In the same way, perhaps it is more helpful to practice forgiveness, at whatever depth and quality is available to that individual's heart at that time, than it is to judge the type and quality of that forgiveness.

ASKING FORGIVENESS FROM ANOTHER

When one person asks forgiveness from another, it is an act of humility. Many issues immediately come to the fore, not the least of which are:

~The one asking for forgiveness may be met with a whole host of other emotions from the one they are asking, and forgiveness may be denied, or postponed while these issues are navigated. This may be conscious on the part of the one you have asked, or it may be largely an unconscious swirl of feelings around the incident and how it is being processed. We will touch on this more in the section on Non-violent Communication and forgiveness later in this book.

~The one you are asking forgiveness from may not know how to forgive. This can be a real problem. You both need to seek help and guidance regarding how best to work through this together. Meher Baba played that role for others, during his lifetime, of facilitating forgiveness – among other things.

~The one you are asking forgiveness from may be so deeply hurt that they have no intention of ever forgiving you, and they may just want to punish you, or lock you out of their life forever. This brings up the title of Don Stevens' book, *The Doorbell of Forgiveness*. What if you ring the bell – request forgiveness – and instead you are ignored, or told to go away? What then?

Of course in a perfect world, when you ask for forgiveness from another you are pardoned, and life with that individual may resume, although the relationship may be substantially changed as a result. Aspen shared with me on this point, "Responsibility and acceptance of our actions have to go hand in hand with forgiveness."[14]

ASKING GOD (OR BABA) FOR FORGIVENESS

This one is particularly personal, as each individual's understanding of God, or their relationship with Meher Baba (or their spiritual master) is unique. This is further complicated by the additional layers of shame and guilt associated with admitting the fault in oneself to this higher power. The vulnerability and honesty, and reality of this type of forgiveness make it extremely powerful, and sometimes quite scary for some. This also sometimes comes to a point where the individual asking for forgiveness feels that God already knows all about the situation, and one's own feelings and needs in the situation. And they may feel that only God truly understands, and only God can truly forgive. This may also be a case where one is not able to communicate with the individual they would like to be able to ask forgiveness from, and so they turn to God instead. Or perhaps they did ask someone to forgive them, but did not get a satisfactory response, and turned to God instead feeling that if God (or Baba) can forgive them then the rest doesn't matter as much.

When I contemplate this, I remember that God is present in all that lives, as the soul of all life. To me, then, when I turn toward God and humble myself asking forgiveness for my weakness, or harm I have caused, there is a mystical sense of asking that of all souls, all beings. Perhaps, although I can't be certain, the relationship I have with God is also maintained as my relationship with that One in all. So, maybe – just maybe – my asking forgiveness from God does reflect on how another soul feels about me, or my behavior.

Regarding how this may bring more peace in my life, I feel that ultimately all my thoughts, words, feelings and actions are between God and myself, and at the end of the day I have to be at peace with God. So, if God and I are on the same page, I can bring that relationship and that peace into all my other relationships. Likewise, if God and I are at odds, and there is no peace with God, naturally that will also be reflected in my other relationships.

FORGIVING GOD (OR BABA) OR A SITUATION

This is a rather common one among the seminar participants I have worked with over the years. It seems that many people actually blame God (or Baba) for whatever circumstances have happened in their lives. It has been quite fascinating to see how this works out in a variety of circumstances. Many people seem to be so angry about something that happened to them in their lives, that they have become a victim in that situation, and for whatever reason they feel the cause of their suffering was in fact God. We will talk more about this in the section on reincarnation, karma and sanskaras.

GOD (OR BABA) FORGIVING A PERSON, GROUP, NATION, OR PLANET.

I just added this direction in here as I contemplated the fact that we do have some indication from Meher Baba (and others) that God is forgiving, what God forgives (or doesn't) and how at least Baba explains that part of the process. I will have a whole section dedicated to what Baba says about God forgiving, and his own style of forgiveness. Aspen responded to this point, "I am very interested in this and would like to see more about it. How can you tell when you are forgiven by God vs. using it as a shield to hide behind – or a cop out of actual forgiveness?"

While I don't believe that one can be certain about when God's forgiveness comes, I do believe we can feel God's Love and Grace and Peace in our hearts. It is for each individual to make peace with God. Eruch said, "Before you even get to the F in Forgiveness, Baba has forgiven you."

AN INDIVIDUAL ASKING A GROUP FOR FORGIVENESS

Once we move out of the personal forgiveness, one to one, we start entering a controversial area, wherein the question can be asked, is it possible that as a "group" there can be forgiveness? For example, can a person ask a group to forgive them? I think yes.

Anyone can beseech a group for forgiveness, and then it is up to that group to determine what that means, and how it can be achieved. I think of a case wherein a person knows that a mistake they made is punishable by a group. They ask for forgiveness from that group, and instead of being punished by the group they are pardoned.

There are two issues that arise from my point of view: The first is, the responsibility of the group. The next is the responsibility of the individual asking a group for forgiveness. It is quite possible that the individual asking for forgiveness, is in fact trying to run from responsibility for their actions, and there is a lesson that comes through the experience of punishment of some type. I think this raises an important question – can the same lesson (and even higher lessons – higher in the sense of more spiritually attuned, or bringing more awareness) be learned through the experience of forgiveness, or do some lessons have to be learned through punishment? I am inclined to believe that the higher experience for all can be accomplished through forgiveness – or else I wouldn't be writing this book. Then again, there are a number of cases where even Meher Baba punished people rather than forgiving them. I can think of a number off the top of my head, but the point is that perhaps in some cases it is actually best to punish. Now as I think of it, the main issue to me is that a God-realized Master, or the Avatar,

FORGIVENESS WITH MEHER BABA

may be able to distinguish when it is best to punish vs. forgive, but for my spiritual path the best way forward is this: Forgive whenever it is possible for me to forgive (in keeping with my core beliefs) and if it is not possible for me, then deal with it in the next best way I know how.

Another issue that comes up is a group using their "forgiveness power poorly." I can think of a group which is not forgiving "for the right reasons," perhaps in the case of a political pardon, or military pardon, where there is no spiritual or emotional content. Or if a group demands something in return for that forgiveness, that may be questionable as well.

AN INDIVIDUAL FORGIVING A GROUP.

Perhaps a Baba lover feels they have been treated unfairly – or unkindly – and they would like to move forward in that community, but cannot do so without some type of group forgiveness first. Forgiving their local Baba Community would be an example of this type of forgiveness.

A GROUP FORGIVING AN INDIVIDUAL

Perhaps a group has found an individual guilty of some offense and instead of punishing that individual decides to forgive them. How this is achieved would be highly personal to the nature of the group and the individual's error.

A GROUP ASKING FORGIVENESS FROM ANOTHER GROUP

Also highly controversial, and I am uncertain as to how this would be accomplished exactly, but for example, could Americans as a group ask for forgiveness from the Native American people regarding how they were treated – being placed on reservations. One of the problems with this type of forgiveness, and this example, is that the behavior being forgiven may still be in full force and effect. Aspen shared, "A distinction may need to be made here between the idea of the group and the individuals that make up the group. As in the 'Group' may forgive but many individuals in the group may not." I think she is right, and this is not the first time I have heard this argument that Group forgiveness is not a reality, for it assumes (or suggests at the very least) that a Group would have to have consensus for this to be a reality. What about "majority rule" and other forms of Group process, one might ask?

This obviously needs deeper contemplation, and I simply say – this is not clear to me, but I want to keep this question alive. Another question which arises is, "Does forgiveness in group dynamics need to be unanimous?"[15] In other words, is a consensus required, or can it be a majority vote, and still be seen as relevant and meaningful in regard to healing?

Another relevant example would be Americans asking forgiveness of Japanese-Americans for the time they were sent to prison camps in America during WWII, even though they had done absolutely nothing wrong, only that they had Japanese heritage.

A third example, and one which I experienced directly was: two Meher Baba groups in the same town, one old and one new, and not communicating because of some differences (or mistakes) made in the past. Can a group ask another group to forgive them?

A GROUP FORGIVING ANOTHER GROUP (OR NATION), ETC.

What is any forgiveness book without mentioning the World War II Holocaust? In this example, is it ever possible that Jews (as a group) can forgive the Nazis (as a group) for the crimes and atrocities committed during the Holocaust, and move on? This brings up an interesting point, in that some would say that the Nazis as a group do not exist any longer (if you do not count the neo-Nazi movements). So the question arises, do both groups need to be currently existing for this to work? This is another level of the one-on-one forgiveness question; do both parties need to be involved for individual forgiveness to work? On this point, Aspen shared, "Personally, I think forgiveness for this is not just. I don't believe that everything must be forgiven, but it can be let go." Some further questions arise now; are there times when something is really unforgivable? We address this more in Chapter Three, "When To Forgive." Also, what happens when something is let go, but not forgiven? Alistair Cockburn speaks to this in his chapter, "Stepping into Loving and Letting Go."

FORGIVENESS AND COMPASSIONATE COMMUNICATION

Right around the time the Forgiveness with Meher Baba seminars started to take off, I was practicing Compassionate Communication (or Non-Violent Communication – NVC) a lot in my personal life. [16]

At that time we created a worksheet for use by the forgiveness seminar participants, based on the four-step NVC process, which briefly described is as follows:

1. Observations: What was the concrete event or incident that happened (words or deeds) that are the source of the need for forgiveness?

2. Feelings: What are your feelings in relation to this event (observation)?

3. Needs: What needs do you have (or values, or desires) which are directly connected to your feelings above?

4. Request: We make a request to meet the need stated above. In the evolution of this NVC process for the forgiveness seminar we created a set of options based on the forgiveness directions, and allow the participant to write directly in the form:

A. I forgive myself for:_____.
B. I forgive _____ for:
_____.
C. Dear _____please forgive me for: _____.
D. Beloved Baba, please forgive me for: _____.
E. Baba, I am upset with you for: _____and I forgive you.
F. Beloved God, please forgive me for: _____.
G. To the _____ group, please forgive me for: _____.
H. To the _____ group, I am upset with you for:
_____ and I forgive you.
I. More forgiveness expressions (you decide): _____.

Keep in mind this worksheet is completed individually in silence, within the group seminar process, and it takes around
thirty minutes. Something about using a paper and pen, and
moving your body to do this work, bringing it down from the
mental emotional storm into words is extremely powerful and
healing and transformative.

We then ask for volunteers to share what they did with the
worksheet, and we process together. It is truly an amazing tool.
We have received tremendous feedback about the usefulness of
this process. We have also heard that the forgiveness seminars
are the most intimacy that some Baba lovers have felt in the
Baba community in years, or even decades.

This return to intimacy, with ourselves, our community, and with God reminds me of a quote from Eruch Jessawala, "The first pang of wrong doing is instructive. When we carry guilt beyond that, we belittle the All-Merciful nature of God."

Carol Verner related that Eruch said this in June 1994 in Mandali Hall.

---

[10] In *All Men are Brothers: Autobiographical Reflections.*

[11] Christie Pearson, at Meherana (January 2014) said to Laurent that Adi K. Irani said (in the 1970s) that Avatar Meher Baba said this to him.

[12] Aspen via editorial notes, June 30, 2015. See also the chapter "A Sample Forgiveness Life-Cycle."

[13] Ibid.

[14] Ibid.

[15] From March 15, 2016 in editorial comments.

[16] For more about NVC see: The Center for Non-Violent Communication here: http://www.cnvc.org.

Chapter Three
When to Forgive?

Forgiveness means giving up all hope for a better past. [17]

ALEXANDER'S PRESENT MOMENT

I remember early on in my conversations with people about this forgiveness work, and the seminars, there were a lot of "Aha!" moments, as this was largely uncharted territory for me. Even though I was working on it regularly there were just layers upon layers of issues and new discoveries almost every month it seemed. That was a very exciting time in my forgiveness-life indeed, and one of my favorite stories has to do with my spiritual brother, Alexander. At that time we were both navigating very similar forgiveness projects in our lives – we had both recently divorced after many years of marriage, and the pain of this was fresh and alive. I remember Alex called me on the phone, and we discussed many aspects of forgiveness when suddenly he had a breakthrough saying essentially – You know, I really have to forgive her because if I don't I am not in the present moment, and I need to be in the present moment, for my own health. He then went on to write to me later, "Holding on to a perceived transgression does not allow one to fully embrace the awareness within the present moment. The act of forgiveness rids one of the burden of holding on to what is not present."

I was stunned. Alex had managed to nail concisely one of the major principles of forgiveness, just naturally and spontaneously in conversation. Lack of forgiveness binds us to the past. Forgiveness, at least in part, frees us from the bindings of the past, and allows us to return, with health and well being, to our own present moment. Wow.

Process vs. Results

Forgiveness may in fact be a long process depending on who is involved and the nature of the problem. Then there are results of this process – the what of forgiveness. Once the process has been lived through fully, the result may be experienced rather suddenly and as uplifting.

As far as I know, no one has the corner on the market of how to forgive and when. There is an important scripture from the life of Jesus that can perhaps shed some light on this issue of process and results and timing. Here is what is attributed to Jesus: [18]

> If therefore when you are offering your gift upon the altar,
> you remember that your brother has a grievance against you,
> leave your gift there before the altar, and go and make
> friends with your brother first, and then return and proceed
> to offer your gift.

This passage from Jesus clearly states that the time to forgive is right now, indeed even before worshiping God. This is worthy of deep contemplation, as it appears Jesus is saying that us all getting along with one another, even loving one another, may be much more important than worshiping an infinite God with gifts at the altar. If that is true then what Don Stevens told me, shortly before he died, has even more meaning: "The most important spiritual work in the world today is that of forgiveness."

Unforgivable: When it Seems Impossible to Forgive.

To be totally honest is not so easy. One of the ways I am honest about forgiveness is to say that sometimes I feel that what someone has done is so vile, so abhorrent, so utterly disgusting to me, that I simply cannot forgive them. It is – to me at least – unforgivable. The action may be forgivable for someone else, but to me I just feel completely stuck and unable to move forward in any loving or forgiving way. Am I wrong to feel that way? Am I not spiritual because I have hit some sort of forgiveness-wall, or area of my own personal issues that I am unable to forgive that individual? I don't know – but what I do know is that I am currently struggling with just such a forgiveness project in my own life, and it is with an individual who has abused someone I love – not me. So now there is a triangle of issues, and the most I have been able to do is try to forgive (using a technique I will share later in the book), and ask Meher Baba to help me to be able to forgive this individual. I feel utterly helpless and hopeless to achieve forgiveness for this individual myself. I am aware of feeling tremendous emotion – anger and hatred – based on what this individual has done in the past, and I struggle with wanting to punish this individual. That is my honest experience. This is a current alive forgiveness struggle, and I share it knowing that it will bring up issues perhaps in the reader.

So, part of the process, seems to be – being able to ask God (or Baba) to help one to just be able to forgive, or ask Baba to help one to want to forgive, and realize that one is far from the state of being able to really forgive wholeheartedly. That is my current experience of this one individual in my life. To sum it up – I am just not there yet with this one person.

This reminds me of one of the Forgiveness with Meher Baba seminars I facilitated at a Meher Baba group in California. I was sharing about my process around my second forgiveness project, and how I struggled deeply with wanting to punish certain individuals for their behavior, but I pushed past that into forgiveness, and felt I had been successful. One of the seminar participants told me privately, during a break after one of the two hour sessions, that my stating so plainly that I wanted to punish someone really pushed his boundaries of what he could hear from me. I listened carefully. I am going to continue to be honest during seminars, and here in this volume about my struggles and conclusions and open questions. I don't pretend to have it all figured out, but I do have some experience now, and I will share that experience.

Meher Baba also shared, more than once, about unforgivable behavior. In these two related quotes, Baba is speaking about how God feels (Baba did that frequently), and it is worth including here as a warning for all in this time of many false masters, or so called "shamans" or guides who have self-interest at heart:

Remember one thing: God is all-merciful. He is eternally in bliss. He cannot forgive one thing, and that is posing. Being a scoundrel, if one pretends to be a saint, God will not forgive it. [19]

And similarly,

The only sin which God does not forgive is hypocrisy. The hypocrite deceives himself and others too. These days the hypocritical saints have increased in such numbers that, though I am the Ocean of Compassion, it has become nauseating even to me! [20]

WHEN TO FORGIVE WITH MEHER BABA'S HELP

This all reminds me of something that Don Stevens said to us during the seminar that is captured in *The Doorbell of Forgiveness* book. Don said,

What are the mechanics of forgiveness? How does it happen? How does real forgiveness happen? And then gradually enough built up and I saw the huge complexity of it. And as I saw the complexity, I said to myself – my God, this is a whole new field for civilization to tackle: to do something about forgiveness itself, and the mechanics of it, and the results of it. And how to improve the efficiency of forgiveness. And I was getting nowhere in trying to dream up any – how do you go about measuring, or what's the methodology of forgiveness? [21]

How can you, some way or another, formulate it? And then tell other people about it or how to go about it and measure its efficiency and how can you improve it?

Then Don told a very long story about a forgiveness project in his own life, and continued with:

And so, this to me, was my confirmation that the intuition that Baba had that the energy and the way, so that if you've got the courage to touch the Doorbell of Forgiveness, by God you link into a circuit where things happen that are incredible... This is why I think forgiveness has Baba's touch, and I can predict that anybody that's got the courage to try it is gonna have something to experience and really be amazed about — working with the Avatar on something that the Avatar has put his heart and soul into. And Baba has done it, I know it. [22]

17 This quote been attributed to both Jack Kornfeld and Lily Tomlin.

18 Book of Matthew, 5:23-24.

19 Ibid, *Lord Meher*, p. 4713.

20 Ibid, *Lord Meher*, p. 5750.

21 See our chapter about "A Sample Forgiveness Life-cycle."

22 *The Doorbell of Forgiveness*, pp. 155-159.

Chapter Four
How to Forgive

Let the past be gone. Why worry about past wrongs?
Every person has done something very wrong ...
God is there to forgive. —MEHER BABA[23]

Forgiveness Seminars

When we started the forgiveness seminars, there was a serious focus on making forgiveness practical and real, not just some unachievable spiritual theory or yummy catch phrase. How forgiveness all began for me is a combination of two main events in my life: a weekend seminar with Don Stevens during 2007, and an interview I conducted with Jean-Paul Samputu (and a later lunch date with him in London). Jean-Paul is a survivor of the Rwandan genocide, and his forgiveness story is one of the most inspiring I have ever heard. [24]

From October 20 – 21, 2007 twelve of us met with Don Stevens at the seventh Young People's Group seminar, with the given theme of forgiveness. This seminar was later transcribed and turned into the book *The Doorbell of Forgiveness*. Don had asked us to do homework, when he said "prepare to discuss forgiveness" before coming to the seminar. I had completed my homework on the AmTrak train ride from Flagstaff to Los Angeles. I reproduce much of it here, just as I shared it that week-end, since it expresses my current feelings on the subject:

> Forgiveness frees the guilty from the bindings of justice. Forgiveness is a gift of love from the more wise to those less kind. Forgiveness is a sacrifice on the altar of conscious-ness whereby the ego can leave behind a piece of itself, sur-rendered to the Highest. Forgiveness is expansive, and touches the wronged, the guilty, and those who bear wit-ness. Individual forgiveness takes one stone off the old wall of separation, while group forgiveness works to remove the entire wall. Forgiveness speaks the language of Oneness, while justice speaks the language of separation. Forgive-ness is unexpected, while justice is Divine Law. Forgive-ness is above the law, and is a divine attribute.

In doing research after the seminar, in preparation for further writing on forgiveness for my chapter in the book, I found these two quotes:

> Who did it? They should come forward and acknowledge their guilt so that I may forgive them. They should not be afraid, because I am Infinite Forgiveness. – Meher Baba [25]

> "The judges of the world bring guilt to the guilty and pun-ish them. I bring guilt to the guilty and forgive them." – Meher Baba [26]

What I find fascinating about these two quotes is that Baba uses the word "guilt" in both of them. In the first one, he seems to indicate that the individual to be forgiven should first acknowledge their guilt before he would forgive them. This is a sentiment that I have heard many times in our forgiveness seminars, that an individual may require that the one they need to forgive should acknowledge their wrong doing, before forgiveness can be granted. Not always, but it is a common theme. Aspen shared with me, "I like that he doesn't dismiss their faults."

Another amazing part of the first quote is that Baba self identifies as "Infinite Forgiveness." I love this, and it is encouraging. This is also confirming to me that forgiveness is indeed a divine attribute. As it turns out Baba said many other things about forgiveness and I will touch upon a few more here, and then dive deeply into his major sharing about forgiveness in the chapter "Forgiveness with Meher Baba."

Here is another quote from Baba on forgiveness:

> Without love, none can cultivate the noble habit of forgetting and forgiving. You forgive a wrong done to you in the same measure in which you love the wrong-doer ... Forgiveness follows love. – Meher Baba [27]

Aspen asked me, "What about forgiving someone you cannot love?" In this quote, Baba is directly tying love to forgiveness. It seems one reason it may be difficult to forgive someone is that you simply don't love them. This may be a chicken and the egg situation. You feel some need to forgive someone you really don't love, but you because you don't love them you can't for-

33

give them. I can relate to this deeply. My solution is to postpone the forgiveness part of the equation and start to cultivate some type of loving attitude towards them first. Then you can revisit your feelings about forgiving them in the light of love. Whew.

During that seminal forgiveness weekend with Don, he shared a number of his forgiveness intuitions, perhaps the most powerful of which is titled simply: "Forgiveness 3" and which reads as follows:

Paris 14 September 2007 8:30am

Forgiveness is the ultimate test of the ego. To condemn is the ultimate declaration of separateness. In this incarnation I have reserved for my true devotees the expression of complete forgiveness, first in their own lives, and then in the teaching to others of the example that they are qualified to make for others. Do not confuse my function in this lifetime with the activity I have included importantly in other lifetimes when my lovers have built religions around my words. As I told the Press in London on my first visit in the 30s, I have not come to establish a new religion in this lifetime, but to revivify the world's existing great religions and gather them together like beads on one string. With my repeated visits with Eruch, as he has recounted to you, and the lengthy work I have done repeatedly at those spots and through other means as well, I have cleansed these and other focal spots of great and sincere veneration from much of the resi-

These "focal spots" are the locations Meher Baba directed Don to visit in India, and film for him, which form the itinerary of the India Beads on One String tour. There are other sites as well.
– LW

due of hate and competitiveness which has so encrusted them, and readied them to be placed side by side in the great fact of Oneness of all Truth.

This basic chore of the scouring of the filth of hate and condemnation, which has been such a constant heritage of the relationships so often rampant between religions, must be completed by my devotees and those others they bring to this central task which I have confided to them in this final period of the last cycle of Avataric cycles. Let there be no mistake; the assignment I give my true devotees is not that of building more churches and receptacles for the bodies of new believers in Meher Baba nor Jesus Christ nor of the Avatars in still other incarnations, but in preparing through forgiveness of the base for true and complete harmony at the deepest levels of feeling and being.

This has never been done before and will take great insight and patience to accomplish. The problem, of course, is the old one that has existed since the beginning of time: that of the "I" and "me" and "mine" of the ego. Just as the great receptacle of the ego becomes that of feeling one has become religious, so the next great refuge so dangerous to the functioning of Truth in the new cycle of Avataric cycles is that the ego will find its haven in the act of condemning those who have deviated in their opinion from the Path of Unity. Instead, they are to be forgiven to allow them their real opportunity to join the surge of true unity that I have made possible in my deep efforts in this direction during my lifetime as Meher Baba.

Do not be confused. True forgiveness is now absolutely necessary to clean out the last dregs of resistance to real Oneness between the great religions themselves, and the reality of this true forgiveness is now to be lived and practised in the world by my devotees as their act of love and devotion to me. There is no other task as central and important as this, which I am entrusting to them and embodying in these words to you. [28]

While we printed this in *The Doorbell of Forgiveness* as well, a few points here in the intuition from Don are worth discussing, which I didn't feel like addressing in that book. The most important point is the tone of the intuition and the fact that it seems to use a voice, which is that of someone other than Don himself. For example, the intuition uses this phrase, "... during my lifetime as Meher Baba." For those who knew Don it comes as little surprise that he may have intuited a message such as this directly from Meher Baba.

Whether it is actually coming over to Don from Baba remains up to the reader to determine, but it stands as one of the most amazing writings we have received from Don to date. Let us look at some other points which are contained in this intuition.

The piece starts off contrasting forgiveness with condemnation. It states that it is a test for the ego to be able to forgive. It also states that condemning is a form of separating. Both of these may seem to be rather obvious, and yet they do add to the conversation. If one is aspiring to overcome the ego life, in favor of a more spiritual life, it would seem that forgiveness is an essential practice. If however, one is not concerned with spirituality and is quite okay with ego-centric living and separative behavior, it seems that condemnation is the "way of the world." As Baba said, bringing guilt to the guilty and punishing them is the way of the world. Spirituality therefore must necessarily be something different, and forgiveness must mean, at least in part, not punishing, and not condemning.

It reminds me again of Jesus, when he comes to the side of the prostitute in the famous story of him saving her from being stoned to death. The result of that story is she walks away, unharmed by the mob, and forgiven by Jesus, who also tells her to give up that way of life. Amazing.

At the time of the YPG seminar, Don wouldn't let us return home without giving us more homework. This time it was to do a "forgiveness project in your own backyard." We knew exactly what he meant. According to Don, we wouldn't get anywhere in this work unless we started at home, and identified an issue which we knew needed forgiveness and tackled it head on, immediately. I took this to heart, and knew what I needed to do – even before we left that seminar: forgive my father for his suicide.

By the time I had accomplished that first forgiveness project, and started to examine the results, I was immediately given more forgiveness work to do. This may sound silly, but it was my experience. And of course, forgiveness flows in many directions, so what I mean is that I was made painfully aware of issues that I felt I needed to address, and forgiveness seemed like a good option at that time. When I speak about my own experience of forgiveness, when conducting seminars, some are triggered or upset when I say that there are times I want to punish someone, but I am choosing to forgive. Is it wrong to feel your feelings first, and then forgive? I speak more about this in the chapter, "A Sample Forgiveness Life-cycle."

How to Speak about Forgiveness

One of the common pitfalls I have experienced in working with groups around forgiveness is the need for conscious language when doing this work together.

For example, I believe it is important to be careful about saying things that start with the phrases "As Baba lovers we should..." or "Baba wants us to..." and etc. In my personal experience, this attempt to speak for the group, using what I call "We" language, can be more divisive than inclusive. During more than ten seminars I have personally facilitated, when I have heard a participant say what they mean using "We" instead of "I" to express themselves, almost invariably they court dissension from the one or many who just don't agree with the statements and don't want to be lumped in with that. This makes those who don't agree uncomfortable, for if they remain silent, they may feel that silence equals consent (or assent), whereas if they speak up and say – "Hey, I don't feel that way at all, actually..." then they risk dividing the group. This is a difficult situation to manage in a seminar, and rather than waste precious energy on divisive language, I recommend always using "I" language whereby each individual takes responsibility for their own feelings and thoughts, rather than projecting them onto the group.

To make this point more clearly, there is a great story from Meher Baba's life, where Lud Dimpfl plays a part in sharing this fundamental lesson. This takes place at Meherabad, India during 1954:

> Two years before, when Lud Dimpfl had met Baba in Myrtle Beach, although he felt happy to meet the Avatar, he felt perplexed as he had not felt touched by Baba in the way so many others had. Now, as he listened to some speak of their feelings of deep love for Baba, he became annoyed. He doubted their sincerity, as he did not feel the same. When it was his turn, he said something about being tongue-tied, but, upon Baba's encouragement, he said, "Baba, I do not know what we are all talking about. We sit here like a bundle of sticks. We do not see you as you are, and here we are all trying to outdo each other like King Lear's daughters as to how many compliments we give you."

> Baba smiled and stated, "Say I, not we."

> Lud thought Baba was displeased with him and said something to that effect, and appeared deeply distressed. Baba reassured him: "I love you and will never be displeased. Speak from your heart. If you hide what you feel, you will not be honest. I love you for being honest. I really love you. Say whatever you feel, but say always I, not we. Do you feel

happy?" Lud replied he did, and Baba stated, "What else is necessary?"[29]

GROUND RULES

Another aspect of doing group forgiveness work is the need for agreed upon ground rules for participants. I offer a short list of them here (I have found long rules do not get absorbed very well anyway):

1. Listen when someone is speaking.

2. Do not offer advice about what someone is sharing unless invited to do so (some of this forgiveness material is very tender and some people have sensitive hearts).

3. If you wish to respond to someone's sharing, perhaps first ask them gently, "Do you want feedback about what you just shared?" and listen for the answer before offering feedback, etc.

MY FEELINGS ABOUT THE FORGIVENESS SEMINARS:

We were invited to facilitate seminars that we had titled Forgiveness with the Christ-Avatar, or sometimes Forgiveness with Meher Baba (depending on the audience). [30]

We held seminars at Meher Baba groups in Sacramento, Los Angeles, Chicago, and Myrtle Beach. All our previous seminars had been less than two days in duration. When we added the extra day, we were able to expand quite a bit the offerings and exercises.

It was wonderful to see so many Baba sisters and brothers attend, as we sat in a circle in the back yard of a Baba-lover's home in Moraga, California I counted 11 women and 11 men. The days were scheduled to have two, two hour sessions each day – so four sessions in total. This pattern of seminar work was the same that Don Stevens instructed me to use and Don and I had traveled around the world using this format, especially for the seminar *Meher Baba's Word & His Three Bridges.*

This forgiveness work was the last work Don asked me to do before he passed away. He particularly asked me to return to a Baba group that was having trouble between the Board of Directors and some of the members, and so I did go there, and it was an amazing seminar.

This new two-day seminar afforded us plenty of time to explore issues around forgiveness in light of Meher Baba's wisdom. I shared firstly some ground rules to help us all feel safe in our sharing together, and I had learned some of the rules from Baba and Don, and some are just common sense. I also asked some questions about what I have come to call the Forgiveness Directions: What does it mean to forgive? How do we forgive another? How do we ask forgiveness? How do we forgive ourselves, and what about forgiving Baba (or God)? How do we ask Baba for forgiveness, or do we just pray the *Prayer of Repentance?* These questions were not intended to be answered in real time, but to be planted as seeds in the participants, and allowed to sprout over the course of the seminar. I was amazed at how quickly the seminar got rolling using this technique.

After we shared a few forgiveness stories, the group jumped right in. Before long we were moving through very tender material coming from all sorts of people in the circle of Baba lovers. In some groups there are one or two who like to share verbally and most are quieter, but here was so much sharing that day one just flew by. At the end of Saturday afternoon, we made it a point to set aside time to do "forgiveness work."

We spent twenty minutes going over some prayers that we can use to tune into the forgiveness flow internally, and also discussed connecting with Baba, in silence, directly. Then we did go into silence – also for about twenty minutes – and when we came out, those who felt moved to share explained what they had done. Baba's presence was palpable to me, as He moved through our hearts within our circle of love. Day two was a similar experience, however there was so much sharing occurring that we broke into smaller groups working in parallel and did not spend time in silence on Sunday afternoon. Instead a co-facilitator spontaneously led the group in a sharing of what each individual "feels they need from their involvement in the Meher Baba community." This was a powerful way for us to close the circle with an intimate intention, and when it was over, many people did not want to leave. I also did forgiveness work during that weekend, and I am grateful for the opportunity I was given to facilitate and participate.

---

[23] Meher Baba to his disciple Baily, in 1919 (In *Lord Meher*, p. 272). For context, Baba received God-realization from Hazrat Babajan between May 1913 – January 1914. See *Lord Meher* p. 197.

[24] See Jean-Paul Samputu's website at http://www.mizero.org/

[25] From *It So Happened*, by William Le Page, p. 59.

[26] From *Lord Meher*, by V.S. Bhau Kalchuri, Vol. 15, p. 5304, (source lordmeher.org accessed September 29, 2010).

[27] From *The Doorbell of Forgiveness* p. 265.

[28] Ibid p. 201, This was from a file given to us by Don titled, "Forgiveness 3."

[29] From *Lord Meher*, pp. 3563-3564.

[30] Many of the early seminars were co-facilitated by Jennifer Brigham. I wish to honor her hard work, intuition and insight, as well as all she shared with me and the participants in those formative days of this seminar. Thank you Soleil.

Chapter Five
Why Forgive? Some Stories

Forgiveness is the most powerful weapon
against terrorism and atrocities. – Jean-Paul Samputu

Jean-Paul Samputu

Shortly after the forgiveness seminar with Don Stevens (at the Young People's Group), Aspen introduced me to the music and spiritual work of Jean-Paul Samputu, in Rwanda. Jean-Paul told me his story during my interview of him for our magazine Om-Point. He is a survivor of the Rwandan genocide in which nearly one million Tutsi tribe members were massacred, including his own parents, brothers and his sister. He knows better than most the need for forgiveness, and so now I will share some of the important points he made to me.

See "Jean-Paul Samputu and the Power of Forgiveness," April 13, 2008 interview by Laurent Weichberger in *OmPoint Circular* #2, p. 18. http://ompoint.com/OmPoint_Circular_2.pdf

I remember the day of our first meeting very well. It was shortly after Don passed away, and I had been asked by people all over the world for information regarding Don's funeral ceremony. In order to reach as many people as possible, I sent an email blast to my entire OmPoint mailing list that the funeral would be held in London, and giving the details. Jean-Paul responded immediately that he was in London and could we get together. So, I literally went from Don's funeral to lunch with Jean-Paul. He recounted exactly what happened in Rwanda, where the two major tribes the Hutu and the Tutsi were involved in one of the worst atrocities in human history.

Jean-Paul's best friend at the time, Vincent (a Hutu) was the one who murdered his entire family, (who were Tutsi). After the genocide, the Hutus including Vincent were caught and imprisoned, as the Hutu government was overthrown. They conducted trials as well, to attempt to bring justice for the survivors.

Jean-Paul told me that when he first discovered that Vincent had killed his entire family, he lost his mind, and left Rwanda, dazed and confused. It took some time for him to get his bearings, because he was suffering so deeply and nothing seemed to cure his mind and heart of the emotional ravages of the genocide. One day Jean-Paul was introduced to a mystical Christian preacher, who helped him process and move through the grief with God, and Jesus and the Bible. After a spiritual awakening, Jean-Paul went on to find Vincent in prison, and forgave him first personally, inside the prison, and later at Vincent's trial. As Jean-Paul explained to me, the judge of the trail asked Jean-Paul directly how Vincent should be punished for murdering Jean-Paul's entire family, and unbelievably he responded – "He should not be punished, I forgive him."

The judge, and all who witnesses this in that courtroom, were naturally astonished. The judge remarked to Vincent, "Then go home now, as Jean-Paul has forgiven you." Then when Vincent returned to his wife and family, his wife said, "If Jean-Paul has forgiven you, so also I forgive you."

That Rwanda genocide trail was so noteworthy, and Jean-Paul's response so moving that the government of Rwanda subsequently bestowed upon Jean-Paul the title: Ambassador of Peace and Forgiveness. Today, Jean-Paul and Vincent are reunited in friendship and actually tour the world together giving forgiveness seminars.

About forgiveness Jean-Paul said to me:

> In the language of Rwanda, known as Kinyarwanda there are two words: "imbabazi" which means (ask for) forgiveness, and "kubabarira" which means to forgive.

> In life we must find creative (or constructive) ways to negotiate conflicts. We cannot change the past but we can change how we approach it, or how we carry our feelings about it into the future, and forgiveness is the key.

> Forgiveness is the most powerful weapon against terrorism and atrocities. To break these cycles of violence, wars, conflicts, is to preach forgiveness. We live in the world where revenge is the culture. Only the culture of forgiveness will stop the cycle (of war, genocide, etc.).

> My real enemy was not the one who wronged me, my real enemy was my hatred, bitterness, my anger which came alive in me. We become what we don't forgive. Forgiveness means to liberate from bondage, to release from the prison of our desire for revenge, of our anger, our bitter-

ness, and hatred. People are not changed by knowing the word of the truth but by living the truth.[31]

LAURENT FORGIVES HIS FATHER AT MEHERABAD

Since I already wrote a blow by blow version of this forgiveness story in *The Doorbell of Forgiveness*, I will simply share here how forgiving my father started me down a path of forgiveness that has lasted so far over eight years. At the time in 2007 when I realized the need to forgive my father, I had no idea what I was doing.

This reminds me a story my dear friend Kelly McCabe once told me:

> A young man decided he needed to go on spiritual pilgrimage to a certain sacred Hindu place. He packed a satchel, put on his sandals and headed out the door of his hut on pilgrimage. At the edge of town a neighbor asked where he was headed, and he told them about his pilgrimage plan. The neighbor responded that it was a great idea, but that the holy place was actually in the other direction. So, the young man turned and headed the way his neighbor pointed. Eventually he found his destination and reached his goal.

I approached forgiveness this way back then. I just did my best to do it. What I discovered along the way is that, like the thoughtful neighbor, there were many spiritual companions along the way to support me in my process. I also found that forgiving my father warmed me up for forgiving others, and turning forgiveness from an event into a way of life. This didn't happen overnight, but more and more, and as I facilitated forgiveness seminars around the country, I realized I was embracing this way more deeply. As Martin Luther King, Jr. once said, "Forgiveness is not an occasional act, it is a constant attitude."

---

[31] On May 19, 2011 in London over lunch, Jean-Paul Samputu, a survivor of the Rwandan genocide, dictated that message for Laurent about forgiveness. Laurent wrote it down, and later sent it to Jean-Paul, who corrected it, and sent it back in its current form.

Chapter Six
Forgiveness and Sanskaras
(including reincarnation and karma)

The sanskaras are not only responsible for the evolution
of the form (body) and the kind of consciousness
connected with it, but they are also responsible
for the riveting of consciousness to
the phenomenal world. – MEHER BABA [32]

AT NEARLY EVERY FORGIVENESS SEMINAR I have facilitated with the
Meher Baba groups, someone will bring up the question, "How
does reincarnation and karma play into all this?" In other
words, based on what we know from Meher Baba about the formation and function of sanskaras, as well as the role of reincarnation and karma in our spiritual unfoldment, are we really
looking at the complete picture of our lives, if we are narrowly
focused on just this life, and the experiences within it. This is a
good question, and an extremely difficult one to address, since
it would take a God-realized master to fully explain to any individual why they are experiencing what they are experiencing
during this lifetime based on their past lives, and the sanskaras
accumulated with the resulting karma in this lifetime.

This reminds me of a story from the life of Meher Baba, and
his meeting with his followers in Myrtle Beach, South Carolina

at the Meher Spiritual Center there in the 1950s. There were three sisters, including my friend Bernice Ivory, who were with Baba in the Lagoon Cabin for a private interview. Because they were black women in the South, before the civil rights movement in America, Baba asked them how they were being treated in the South, during their visit from New York. One of the sisters said something like – You know Baba, it's difficult for us especially in the South. Baba then indicated that the three of them had been white slave-owners who mistreated their slaves in a past-life, and that is why in this life they were black and had to endure the current prejudice in America.

It is interesting to note that during the summer of 1956, when Meher Baba reached South Carolina on a train from New York, when he disembarked onto the railway platform, he had to use a restroom. He found not two but three at the station, "Men, Women," and "Colored." Baba used the Colored restroom to urinate.

This took place just a few months after the home of Martin Luther King, Jr. was bombed. See *Lord Meher* p. 4015.

Since Meher Baba has written at great length about sanskaras, reincarnation and karma in his seminal works *God Speaks* and *Discourses*, we will not cover those topics here, except to summarize for those unfamiliar with the concepts so that we can treat the topic of forgiveness in light of these issues afterwards.

SO, WHAT ARE SANSKARAS (IMPRESSIONS) EXACTLY?

The word "sanskara" is an ancient Hindi/Sanskrit word which has been little understood in Western mysticism until recently. According to Meher Baba, sanskaras are literally impressions in the mental fabric of a living being. A living being, as defined by Baba, is any form in Creation that is evolving towards full consciousness and awareness, and in his cosmology this process starts with cosmic gases, then stones, and metals, and culminates in the human form.

This mental fabric of which Baba speaks, is not the same as the brain, because the physical body with it's brain is only a physical manifestation of the soul. According to Baba there are actually three bodies, a mental body, a subtle (energy) body, and a physical body. The mental body is not dependent on the brain, but uses the brain.

When the physical body dies, the corresponding subtle and mental bodies do not die – they simply dissociate from that particular form. In fact – the soul continues to associate with the subtle and mental body, in an afterlife until it is the right time for that soul to reincarnate. This explanation from Baba gives rise to his comprehensive explanations about the importance of the impressions gathered during the physical lifetime, and how they ultimately need to be balanced (or worked out) in order for the soul to achieve a state of Self-realization. This is a long story, and as we said earlier, one we can't tell properly in this chapter. We can however speak about these subjects just enough to consider them in light of forgiveness. Let's try.

What is reincarnation?

Again from Meher Baba's wisdom, we are told that prior to human form, there is no reincarnation, but rather – evolution. The forms prior to the human form are taken in succession through the various "kingdoms" of Creation which Baba orders as gas > stone > metal > vegetable > worm > fish > bird > animal > human. Upon reaching human form, according to Baba, there is no more evolution, because the purpose of evolution was to achieve a human form. Now that a human form is available, the only work left to do in order to achieve full Self-realization is to disburden the mind of the accumulated impressions from the journey of the soul through the kingdoms of evolution. The impressions Baba speaks of generally as: lust, greed, anger, etc. However, to be more clear, he gives example of impressions gathered in both pre-human and human lifetimes, and how they get worked out. The working out of these impressions, to achieve balance and Self-realization of the human being he terms "reincarnation and karma," and then he proceeds to explain why we need a spiritual master to help us overcome this spiritual dilemma.

Okay then, how does karma work?

Meher Baba was clear that the working of karma requires the soul to take more than one human lifetime. So, from his perspective, what is done in one lifetime requires a subsequent lifetime to balance out. This is not an endless process however, for ultimately the soul reaches a point of spiritual maturity where it no longer blindly acts out the drive and wishes of the ego, but rather strives to overcome all egoistic behavior and disburden once and for all the sanskaric load. This, Baba says, is the entering into the spiritual path, and a process he terms as *involution* of consciousness.

During the reincarnation and karma, and involution of consciousness, there are experiences of life – which are intended to bring harmony and balance to the conscious mind. Throughout his life, Baba gave many examples of the working out of the spiritual law of karma, and each story was in relation to mental (experiential) balance. The assumption was that (in most cases) the balance required from an experience in one lifetime had to be achieved in the next lifetime, unless one managed to realize God and end the cycle of reincarnation and karma for good. This is a daunting goal, and a difficult thing to write about for someone who does not experience the goal, so I am just sharing my understanding of what Baba explained to us in his literature, and the oral tradition.

Baba sometimes used dramatic language to make his point clear, such as this conversation with the notable Buddhist, Mr. Christmas Humphreys, and others during 1931 in London, England:

Baba explained:

> "[In Sufi terms] religion has four aspects: shariat, tariqat, marefat and haqiqat. Man has to go beyond shariat – the external aspect. The Muslims consider it unlawful to go beyond shariat. Yet a Sadguru [Perfect Master] has such powers that if he wishes, he can make a person God-realized in a minute!"

Baba looked at one of the visitors who after listening to Baba's statement was deep in thought. Baba asked him what he was thinking. The man questioned, "How is it possible for a person to gain Realization within a minute?"

Baba elaborated, "Even within a second, all actions can be annihilated and the experience of God instantly given. Bondage to maya [illusion] is always there and karma [bondage] is due to actions. After the actions are destroyed, there is no bondage. Do you think you can obtain Realization in this birth?"

The man replied, "I cannot agree with your statement about karma. How could the effects of actions be done away with in one lifetime?"

"Why not?" Baba smilingly replied. "They can be destroyed by the grace of the Master. If that is not so, of what use is the guru? What is the value of grace if everyone has to await his turn and time?"[33]

Christmas Humphreys was profoundly impressed by meeting Baba and wrote an article titled "The Incarnation of Love," from which I quote:

For the first time in my life, and I have not met another like him, I found myself in the aura of a man who literally radiated love ... He combined the profundity of mystical experience with the guileless candor of a child, and his smile was as infectious as the words he used were immaterial ... And all the while he radiated such a pure affection that one wondered why, when all religions praise the value of pure love, should it be a memorable experience to meet one man who practiced it. If there were more Meher Baba's in the world today, war would end for want of causes. This man of love sets all men an example!

TAKING RESPONSIBILITY FOR OUR PART IN THE SITUATION IN LIGHT OF KARMA.

So how does forgiveness relate to all of that? If what Baba is saying is true, the whole notion of who is the victim and who is the abuser is elucidated by the possibility that all of these experiences are somehow required to be worked out, and balance the mind on the path back to Self-realization and God consciousness.

As you can imagine, also, I have had to avoid this part of the conversation during Forgiveness with Meher Baba seminars, since it brings up a whole host of issues which can be quite charged or tender. Someone who has been a victim of abuse – whether physical, sexual, mental or otherwise – rarely wants to discuss how their past life actions contributed to their need to be abused in this present life to balance out their karma and sanskaras. Only a spiritual master can properly discuss this with anyone, and for followers of a spiritual master to speak that way to each other, while trying to forgive each other and heal is a razor's edge conversation to be sure. That said, it is worth examining in the comfort of a book, and the ability to put the book down at any moment and contemplate:

Is it possible that in a past lifetime, I did something to someone that caused me to have to experience what I just experienced in this lifetime that is bringing up the need for forgiveness?

If so, an inner dialogue, and perhaps some conversation in a safe environment, such as a circle of spiritual companions (as described by Don Stevens), or a therapist of some type, could help that exploration to continue along fruitful lines.

I know at least one Meher Baba follower, who shared a story with me and made it abundantly clear that a particular incident they had experienced in this lifetime was directly related to their own behavior in a recent past lifetime. This helped them to forgive the person involved in the present.

At another time, during our 2007 seminar with Don Stevens, he shared one of his experiences about tenderness:

> ... I don't know whether I was having a simple dream, or whether I was in a semi-awake state, but I found myself in a long, long white hall – no sign of any sort of illumination – no lights – but it was just beautifully, tenderly, simply white. And Baba was to my right. And he was holding my right hand with his left hand. And we were walking down the long white hall. And at the end of it, I didn't ask myself well how'd he get there, how'd I get here with him, what's this all about? I just knew that something important was happening. We walked along. And at the end of this long white hall, on the left hand side, I saw an open door. And

as I saw that open door, I knew, in that room, God is sitting. And Baba is going to take me to see God.

As I walked along the corridor with Baba, and started coming reasonably close to the door, it was just like a tsunami. An absolutely incredible wave completely knocked my whole being into a flip of tenderness. And for some reason or another, I could even identify what that tenderness was all about. And it was tenderness for the human who had to desert the beauty of Oneness and peace and Reality in order to go into this tremendously trying thing of Creation for the sake of God to be able to love. Because that demanded what baba has said to us: For love there has to be a lover and a beloved. And if God is the lover, or if I am the lover, then there has to be separation for love to express itself. [34]

I think that experience of Don's with Baba and the doorway to God's presence is a fascinating contemplation on the role of tenderness in human interaction. Perhaps it is a prescription for living a more tender and loving life in general, that would thereby decrease all actions that are less than loving? I don't know, but I share it because I believe Don is onto something when he reminds us of God's tenderness for struggling humanity.

---

[32] In *Discourses* (6th Edition online), "The Types of Meditation IV," Volume II, p. 141. See: http://discoursesbymeherbaba.org/v2-141.php.

[33] In *Lord Meher* pp. 1274-1275.

[34] *The Doorbell of Forgiveness* pp. 176-177.

Chapter Seven
Forgiveness and Surrender

The only Real Surrender is that in which poise is
undisturbed by any adverse circumstance,
and the individual, amidst every kind of hardship,
is resigned with perfect calm to the will of God.
—MEHER BABA[35]

THIS QUOTE BEGS THE QUESTION, what is the relationship between forgiveness and surrender? It is clear from what Baba
says that adverse circumstances, and hardships, can be deeply
disturbing. Also, he gives an antidote to this suffering in form of
resignation to the "will of God," or surrender. This is a tough
one for many in the West.

When one experiences adversity and hardship at the hands of
another individual, such as direct abuse, it automatically brings
into play the role of forgiveness. Is forgiveness then another
type of surrender or resignation to the will of God? I have been
asked by Aspen to say more about this question. Another way of
asking this is, Does my attitude in any given situation proclaim
"this behavior is unacceptable," or can I be tolerant of this behavior? If a forgiving attitude helps me to be more tolerant and
accepting of what is, rather than trying to change it, this is a
type of surrender to the will of God. Lately, I have started to

practice expanding my circle of tolerance, and reducing my circle of what is unacceptable.

This shifts my attention away from the question of the wrong done, and towards the perspective of – why am I here again, anyway? In other words, what is the purpose of my soul's journey, and did that perceived wrong in some way free me, or release me, or send me in a different life-direction which is in fact closer to the core, or truth, of who I really am, and who I am meant to be?

When reflecting on the largest challenges in my life to date (I am now 47), I think of the suicide of my father, which when I tackled that wholeheartedly led me to my spiritual path with Meher Baba. And the other would be the betrayal I experienced which led to my divorce, and the breakup of my family, after almost two decades, and set me into a New Life with Baba and lots of unexpected experiences.

If I apply the definition above from Baba about surrender, and surrender my dad's suicide, and surrender the divorce, I am resigned to Baba's Will for me, and I do sleep well at night. If, instead, I obsess, or fume, or feel justified in my anger, I experience the adversity as "unjust" or "unfair" or whatever, and go into all kinds of thoughts and feelings, none of which are particularly spiritual or practical. And then I realize, wait – I have a choice. This reminds me of another thing Baba said, "When you are in the garden, you can either focus on the bugs or on the flowers." I choose to focus on the flowers in my life, and ignore the bugs (as much as possible). Aspen lovingly reminds me, "Bugs help flowers grow, and without them there would be no garden."[36]

Accepting the bugs as Baba's will, and delighting in the flowers is my simple approach which is connected to surrender, and also helps me to forgive. It is also closer to the truth that we are essentially all one, and this daily experience of mine is more like a dream, which when I awaken, I will fully realize was not the Reality.

---

[35] See "The Seven Realities of Meher Baba's Teaching" in *Discourses*, by Meher Baba online at http://www.discoursesbymeherbaba.org/v1-15.php

[36] Edits from Aspen, March 5, 2016.

Chapter Eight
Forgiving the Dream

WHAT IF THIS REALLY IS ALL ILLUSION, and my soul's dream created by Maya? What if all the wrongs and hurts and adversities and pain I endure are really dream experiences, and when I wake up I will be whole, and complete, and unharmed? Aspen responded to this question with, "If it is, does it change anything at all?" To which I can simply say, "Yes, it changes my attitude."

During 1956 in Los Angeles, California, Meher Baba once explained:

> All this is nothing but a dream. When you are asleep, you find yourself talking, enjoying, sometimes you weep, sometimes you are happy; but when you are awake, you realize the pain and joy that you felt in the dream were nothing but a dream.

> Even this is a dream – your sitting with me. The noise of the buses and street cars, this place, the whole city, all of this is nothing but a dream.

Suppose tonight in a dream, you see Baba sitting beside you and explaining, "Don't get entangled in all of this, it is nothing but a dream," then you would question me, saying, "Baba, how could it be a dream? I have so many joys and sorrows. I see so many people around me. I see you. How could it be a dream?" The next day, you wake up and you realize that Baba appeared to you in a dream and said it was but a dream.

Even now, at this moment, I tell you that you are dreaming. But how does your mind react? You say, "Baba is with us, how could everything be a dream?" Then I say: "When you realize Reality, when you are wide awake after Realization, you will realize all that I said is true – that it was all nothing but a dream."

Try to make the best of this contact with me by loving me more and more.[37]

So, if what Baba is saying is correct, and I am in fact dreaming my relationships, dreaming my joy and my sorrow, dreaming the adversity and the triumph, then I have mistaken my dream for reality. Perhaps, then, my forgiveness work will help me awaken from the dream, and not take the dream so seriously?

May it be so.

---

[37] *Lord Meher* pp. 4061-4062.

Chapter Nine
Forgiveness and Substance Abuse

I HAPPEN TO BELIEVE THAT THIS SUBJECT could become a whole book unto itself, for it is extremely complicated once you bring into a forgiveness con-
versation the two elements of alcoholism, or
substance abuse, and the type of emotional
and physical abuse that one acts out under
the influence. It is also related to the area we
touched upon elsewhere namely, When is it not time to forgive?
There were times in Meher Baba's own life when he did not forgive someone, but punished them for their behavior. In the case
of alcoholism, or drug abuse, sometimes allowing an addict or
alcoholic to experience the consequences of
their behaviors, and not protect them, or shield
them is the best course of action. Aspen asked
at this point, "What about the line between
forgiveness and enabling? How do you forgive
without letting go of the need for the [alcoholic] to have repercussions for their actions?"

See the chapter "Forgiveness and Trauma" by Randy Overdorff.

Substitute addict for alcoholic, or whatever word is best.

In order to respond to this, I asked Vanessa to chime in since she has more current experience with this than I do. She responded with this:

The most important part of the process for someone who is dealing with an alcoholic is to let the alcoholic experience life's natural repercussions for their actions. If those repercussions have to be enforced by me, that act in itself is an act of love because it is an act of justice which allows for the forgiveness process to continue. It is a step in the process, because sometimes the experience of being with an alcoholic can go on for years and years, and the damage can accumulate. And so when you step out of the way and allow for natural repercussions and have to take measures yourself, then the healing in ones own being can start to take place – towards forgiveness.[38]

A few words should be said about Twelve Step groups (such as AA/NA). As Randy wrote, in *Forgiveness and Trauma*, sometimes a traumatized, or deeply wounded person is just not ready to engage the forgiveness process with the one who has wounded them. It may take a long time, or not even in this lifetime, before they are prepared to have further contact, or when further contact would actually make the situation worse rather than better. That can be deeply sad and intense for all concerned. At that point the other techniques we have shared here, such as "Ho'oponopono" come into the picture more clearly.

See Joe DiSabatino's chapter "Wounds, Healing and the Path of Forgiveness."

Step nine of the twelve steps speaks to this point,[39] and although the word forgiveness is not directly used in the twelve steps language, there are steps which seem to require forgiveness at some level:

Step 8: Made a list of all persons we had harmed, and became willing to make amends to them all.

Step 9: Made direct amends to such people wherever possible, except when to do so would injure them or others.

So while "making amends" may be different from "forgiveness work," I am certain they are related. While doing forgiveness work we would do well to contemplate how to make amends, and while making amends those in a twelve steps group process practice forgiveness work as well.

Vanessa and I have been reading out loud together from *Courage to Change*, which is an Al-Anon book, and we have found it to be extremely encouraging, and helpful. Al-Anon is a twelve step support group for the families and friends of those directly connected to alcoholics. As Vanessa shared with me, "Being able to have a focus – which is a solution to letting go of what is holding me back, and to instill new ways of thinking and operating which will help me detach and find a new way of life has been invaluable." This morning we read from the March 15 daily reading, and it was about forgiveness. I wanted to share the most inspiring part here:

Today I know that forgiveness has nothing to do with power. It does not give me control. Forgiveness is simply a reminder that I am on equal footing with every other child of God. We all do good and noble things at times; on other occasions we may offend. I have no right to judge, punish, or absolve anyone. When I behave self-righteously, I am the one who suffers – I separate myself from my fellow human beings, focus on others, and keep busy with hateful and negative thoughts. By taking this attitude I tell myself that I am a victim, so I remain a victim. The most forgiving thing I can do is to remember that my job is not to judge others, but to think and behave in a way that lets me feel good. [40]

---

[38] Sitting with Vanessa in Myrtle Beach, March 26, 2016.

[39] See http://www.aa.org/assets/en_US/smf-121_en.pdf

[40] From *Courage to Change*, p.75 © 2016 Al-Alon Family Groups, Inc.

Chapter Ten
Forgiveness with Avatar Meher Baba

I am the Ancient One, and I have the
divine authority to forgive anyone of anything!
— MEHER BABA [41]

IN THIS CHAPTER WE WILL EXPLORE Meher Baba's relationship to
forgiveness. I want to start by explaining that while Baba obviously had strong feelings about forgiveness, he didn't include it
as a chapter in his major literary works *Discourses*, or *God Speaks*. After some careful
research in *God Speaks*, I found that section
called "Forgetfulness." In this section, after
discussing in depth and detail the meaning of
"positive forgetfulness" and its spiritual value,
Baba concluded:

Look for Supplement
Part 2: Practical Mysticism,
Forgetfulness.

Positive forgetfulness, then, is the cure, and its steady
cultivation develops in man that balance of mind which
enables him to express such noble traits as charity, forgiveness, tolerance, selflessness and service to others. [42]

Speaking of the noble trait of tolerance, it was recently
brought to my attention by my excellent therapist, Asha, that

part of my trouble lies in the fact that I have a large circle of what is "unacceptable." She told me that rather than trying to change anyone else, all I need to do is make my circle of what is unacceptable smaller. This to me is directly related to forgiveness, since in the case I was discussing with her, I was trying to navigate an issue which I felt needed forgiveness and work. She reframed it for me in such a way that I realized after the session, that when Baba speaks about tolerance as a "noble trait," or a virtue, it goes deeper, in that when I make my circle of what is unacceptable smaller, I increase my tolerance. When I increase my tolerance, there is less to forgive. I was never able to relate to tolerance as charity until right now.

Speaking to this point of tolerance, Baba also said,

> If man wants to remain happy, let him be more aggressive towards himself and much more tolerant towards others. This is no cowardice, it is real strength of the brave.[43]

Suddenly, it is clear to me that tolerance undercuts the need for many aspects of forgiveness, like a short circuit. I am going to be practicing tolerance and forgiveness simultaneously now, as a new life experiment.

I also found (and people shared with me over the years) quotes from Baba on forgiveness, and one of the most important insights came directly from Baba's sister, Mani, who was undoubtedly one of the closest disciples (Mandali).

Mani explains Baba's gesture

Baba's sister Mani explained that Baba had "one gesture for two words; there was one gesture for love and for forgiveness, same gesture." Mani demonstrated on a video how Baba made this gesture, reaching down with her hands just below the solar plexus and up towards the heart, and then pushing both hands down and out towards the recipient. She continued, "And when Baba would say 'I forgive you' it seemed like such an oceanic gesture. As if the ocean waters have come over, and that wave has come over to the beach, and receded leaving not a trace..."[44]

When we did the Forgiveness with Meher Baba seminar, invariably we would bring up this point, and demonstrate it for those gathered. On a number of occasions, we would invite the seminar participants to put aside their pens and papers, and instead of sharing and listening, to also perform the gesture, exactly the way that Mani described. The results were unexpected. For some, the fact that Baba's gesture for love and forgiveness were the same was extremely profound. Because of this, we would pause here and ask: what does it mean that Baba's gesture for forgiveness and for love are the same?

This alone would usually create a conversation among the participants, since there is no one right answer. This is a worthy contemplation. One of the best answers I ever heard was when a female co-facilitator shared: "Perhaps it means that, like Baba, we should keep loving someone even though they made a mistake, and so forgiveness means you continue to love them."

So now I ask you, the reader, to perhaps take a moment to contemplate as well: what does it mean that Baba's gesture for Love and for Forgiveness were the same?

I know that since I have started facilitating the Forgiveness with Meher Baba seminar, I have adopted this way of living forgiveness – Keep loving them, as Meher Baba keeps loving us, regardless of our behavior. With few exceptions, which I won't go into here, I have felt this is the best way for me to live this message. That said, I know at least a few stories off the top of my head where Baba punished someone for their behavior, and so it remains our decision always – whether or not to forgive. Otherwise, like love, what is the value in loving if it is forced? I actually believe that is the whole purpose of "free will." Without the gift of free will, how could we ever love God, or love each other? We must have the experience of free will, even if it is just an illusory or dreamlike free will.

BLAMING BABA

This brings up the point that many have shared with me, that during their lives with Baba they just get plain angry with Baba. They blame Baba for their life circumstances, they feel Baba is doing it to them, or they have elaborate and painful stories about how it all fits together – Baba, their suffering, their choices, what Baba wants for them, and on and on. Aspen adds, "Suffering is often part of growth."

This reminds me of what Arnavaz, one of Baba's Mandali, said: "When I see someone who is upset with Baba, I tell that person to repeat over and over – 'Baba, I am angry with you, and I am sorry. Please forgive me and help me to resign to Your wish and will.'"[45]

LOOSENING THE BINDINGS OF DUALITY IN MAYA

There are many stories about Meher Baba's life, and what he said in silence. Some of the most important things we have from Baba he gave out to his disciples and followers in the way of messages or the few books he created, and some are part of the oral tradition, or have been captured in books about him. Here is one of my favorites, which he gave to Don Stevens for the book which became *Listen, Humanity*:

> Forgiveness consists in loosening the bindings of duality in maya, which makes you feel and find the One as many. Therefore 'I forgive you' amounts to the loosening of your bindings. Although it takes a lot of time to build a big stack of hay, a single lighted match can burn all of it in no time at all. Similarly, regardless of the accumulated dirt and refuse of sins, divine forgiveness burns them away in no time.[46]

Here Baba has invoked the problem of Maya, and how this experience of duality is a binding on consciousness, keeping the individual from experiencing the Oneness of God. This is Baba directly encouraging one and all to forgive in order to become free of the ignorance that causes the feelings of separation. He goes on to explain that beyond personal forgiveness is "Divine Forgiveness," which the Masters and the Avatar can use to burn away the impressions (sanskaras) of their followers.

So, we can do our part in becoming free by loving and forgiving more, and it seems the Avatar does his part by forgiving us, amongst all the other things he does, so that we can be free of bindings.

Then there was this very touching story of a man who attended a sahavas with Baba:

> When Baba completed the arrangements for the fast, a gentle-faced man, perhaps fifty years old, rose from among the group and asked permission to deliver some Sanskrit verses. Receiving permission to do so, he recited them so feelingly that apparently the stream broke the flood gates of his heart. He burst into tears, cried out "Avatar Meher Baba ki jai" and asked forgiveness for his sins. Baba motioned the desolate figure into his arms, embraced him warmly, stroked his shoulder and his damp cheeks tenderly and then held him quietly to his chest. "Don't be afraid," he said. "You need not tell me anymore. If I am the Avatar, then I know everything, and everything will be forgiven. If I am not the Avatar, what good will it do you to tell me anything, and what use would it be to ask my forgiveness?" "Christ often said, 'I forgive you, I forgive you'. Those who loved Christ accepted His Prasad (offering) of forgiveness. But those who would not recognize Christ naturally could not understand Him. His words were just words to them.[47]

Meher Baba frequently referred to Jesus Christ, and explained much about his life that most people don't know, such as details about his life after the crucifixion. Baba declared that Jesus and some disciples left Israel and went to live in India. For example, it is common knowledge that the apostle Thomas settled in what is today Tamilakam, India, and converted many there to Christianity. [48] Baba indicated that Jesus went further north and settled in what is today Kashmir.

Baba also revealed the deeper meaning of the words of Christ, and lived them. Mother Theresa said to some followers of Baba that Meher Baba was a Christ-like man. She asked that her statement not be repeated until after she died, as she was a Catholic nun and didn't want to cause any trouble.[49]

During what is known as Meher Baba's New Life where he wandered India with his spiritual companions, on November 24, 1949 in India, Baba said:

> I ask the most merciful God to forgive me and my companions for any shortcomings and any conscious and unconscious mistakes done singly or wholly or toward each other... I forgive you, my companions, and ask you all to forgive me, and I ask God to forgive us all, not merely by way of ceremony but as a whole-hearted pardon.[50]

So here, we can see Baba using the phrase "wholehearted pardon" in regard to forgiveness. Let's look more closely at the word pardon: "an act of officially saying that someone who was judged to be guilty of a crime will be allowed to go free and will not be punished."[51] What is also interesting in this statement from Baba is his use of the words "shortcomings" and "conscious or unconscious mistakes." These are obviously different, the former being about the character of an individual, and the latter being about a mistake made, whether consciously or unconsciously. We can become more aware, and make fewer mistakes, but it is extraordinarily difficult to deal with defects of character.

How do we change personal flaws, defects, and weaknesses? As Aspen asked me, "What is the role of personal humility in forgiveness?" This is a question worthy of contemplation. This seems to all be the work of many lifetimes. I think this is where we see the link between compassion and forgiveness. The more we can realize that we all have some degree of unconscious behavior, conscious mistakes in judgment or words, some character flaws, and worse – the more we can be loving and forgiving in the Light of God's Infinite Forgiveness.

This segues perfectly to one of the most important pieces that Meher Baba has given the world, the Prayer of Repentance. So, while Baba may not have written about forgiveness in his main published works, and there is still more research to do about all he said and did during his lifetime on these subjects, we know for certain that he was extremely serious about the importance of this prayer. I share it here in its entirety so that we can reflect on it later, and see what Baba means by forgiveness in this context. If there is one statement from Baba that will live on regarding forgiveness, this will surely be the one.

THE PRAYER OF REPENTANCE

WE REPENT O GOD MOST MERCIFUL, for all our sins. For every thought that was false or unjust or unclean. For every word spoken that ought not to have been spoken. For every deed done that ought not to have been done. We repent for every deed and word and thought inspired by selfishness. And for every deed and word and thought inspired by hatred. We repent most specially for every lustful thought, and every lustful action, for every lie, for all hypocrisy, for every promise given, but not fulfilled, and for all slander and backbiting. Most specially also, we repent for every action that has brought ruin to others, for every word and deed that has given others pain, and for every wish that pain should befall others.

IN YOUR UNBOUNDED MERCY, we ask you to forgive us, O God, for all these sins committed by us; And to forgive us for our constant failures to think and speak and act according to your wish.

This prayer was given by Meher Baba on November 8, 1952.

Of course, the first part of the prayer is all the ways we can miss the mark in our life. It is a rather comprehensive list of less-than-wondrous behaviors, and enough to give even a good person pause for contemplation. Baba said it was helpful, when praying this prayer, to bring to mind the behaviors done in that spirit, to help iron them out and not repeat them again. In any case, I offer it here for the ending especially. When we can ask God wholeheartedly to forgive us for such behaviors, how does this change us, the one who prays. As a wise person once said, "My prayers don't change God, they change me."

Another side effect of such repentance and self-reflection is that it can lead to worrying about our character, and self-loathing or low self-esteem. That isn't good either. It seems to be a bit of a pendulum swing between feeling love with Meher Baba, and being able to love and forgive others, and then feeling less than great about oneself and struggling with self-loathing or other issues of this type. Baba has something to offer here as well:

I love you.
Do not worry about your weaknesses.
Eventually they will go.
Even if they linger, love will one day consume them.
Everything disappears in the Ocean of Love.
Because I love you,
you have a pool of love within you.
When you feel wretched,
when you fall in your weakness,
have a dip in that pool of love.

Refresh yourself in that pool of my love within you.
It is always there.
Even if you wash your weaknesses every day in that pool,
it will remain clear.
Don't worry. Baba loves you.
That is what really matters. [52]

Someone may say at this point, okay okay, I get the gist of what Baba felt about forgiveness. But is there anything more? There is. The following message from Meher Baba appeared in the 1960s. It is about as comprehensive a statement as exists in the literature, beyond the prayers and quotes sprinkled around here and there.

FORGIVE AND FORGET

People ask God for forgiveness. But since God is everything and everyone, who is there for Him to forgive? Forgiveness of the created was already there in His act of creation. But still people ask God's forgiveness, and He forgives them. But they, instead of forgetting that for which they asked forgiveness, forget that God has forgiven them, and, instead, remember the things they were forgiven — and so nourish the seed of wrong-doing, and it bears its fruit again. Again and again they plead for forgiveness, and again and again the Master says, I forgive.

But it is impossible for men to forget their wrong-doings and the wrongs done to them by others. And since they cannot forget, they find it hard to forgive. But forgiveness is the best charity. (It is easy to give the poor money and goods when one has plenty, but to forgive is hard; but it is the best thing if one can do it.)

Instead of men trying to forgive one another they fight. Once they fought with their hands and with clubs. Then with spears and bows and arrow. Then with guns and cannon. Then they invented bombs and carriers for them. Now they have developed missiles that can destroy millions of other men thousands of miles away, and they are prepared to use them. The weapons used change, but the aggressive pattern of man remains the same.

Now men are planning to go to the moon. And the first to get there will plant his nation's flag on it, and that nation will say, It is mine. But another nation will dispute the claim and they will fight here on this earth for possession of that moon. And whoever goes there, what will he find? Nothing but himself. And if people go on to Venus they will still find nothing but themselves. Whether men soar to outer space or dive to the bottom of the deepest ocean they will find themselves as they are, unchanged, because they will not have forgotten themselves nor remembered to exercise the charity of forgiveness.

Supremacy over others will never cause a man to find a change in himself; the greater his conquests the stronger is his confirmation of what his mind tells him – that there is no God other than his own power. And he remains separated from God, the Absolute Power.

But when the same mind tells him that there is something which may be called God, and, further, when it prompts him to search for God that he may see Him face to face, he begins to forget himself and to forgive others for whatever he has suffered from them. And when he has forgiven everyone and has completely forgotten himself, he finds that God has forgiven him everything, and he remembers Who, in reality, he is.[53]

---

[41] *Lord Meher*, p. 5485.

[42] *God Speaks*, by Meher Baba, pp. 200-201 (Walnut Creek: Sufism Reoriented, 1997).

[43] "Meher Baba's Words from the Diary of Eruch Jessawala," *Glow International*, Fall 2015, p. 4, copyright © 2015 Beloved Archives, Inc.

[44] Mani on Baba's gesture for love and forgiveness being the same, *Doorbell of Forgiveness,* "Forgiveness at Meherabad," p. 251.

[45] *Gift of God*, by Arnavaz Dadachanji, p. 234.

[46] *Listen, Humanity*, by Meher Baba, (Don E. Stevens editor), p. 68.

[47] Ibid p.68.

[48] For more on Thomas see:
https://en.wikipedia.org/wiki/Thomas_the_Apostle

[49] Speak to Mimi Hay, who told me the entire story of her and Erica Hodgin's meeting with Mother Teresa in India and what transpired. I have lost my notes from that conversation.

[50] *Lord Meher*, p. 3501.

[51] According to the Merriam-Webster dictionary on-line.

[52] *Gift of Love*, p.v.

[53] *The Everything and the Nothing* (Meher House, 1967), pp. 109-110, © 2016 Avatar Meher Baba Perpetual Public Charitable Trust.

Life-Cycle of
FORGIVENESS

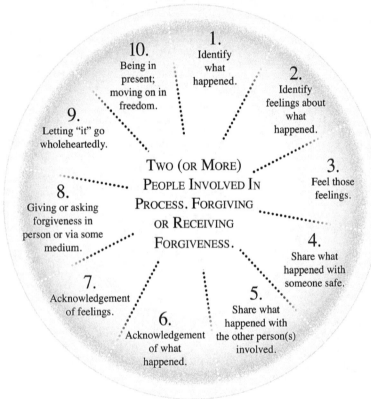

10.
Being in present; moving on in freedom.

1.
Identify what happened.

2.
Identify feelings about what happened.

9.
Letting "it" go wholeheartedly.

TWO (OR MORE) PEOPLE INVOLVED IN PROCESS. FORGIVING OR RECEIVING FORGIVENESS.

3.
Feel those feelings.

8.
Giving or asking forgiveness in person or via some medium.

4.
Share what happened with someone safe.

7.
Acknowledgement of feelings.

5.
Share what happened with the other person(s) involved.

6.
Acknowledgement of what happened.

Chapter Eleven
A Sample Forgiveness Life-Cycle

Forget the past, and make the most of the present.
Keep your own hearts clean. Learn to love each other
first before you tell others about my love for one and all.
Give love, receive love, gather love; everything
else is dissolved eventually in the truth of
divine love. – Meher Baba[54]

This chapter is dedicated to a simple diagram I was inspired to create after being asked a question by Randy Overdorff at the Meher Spiritual Center: "What is the difference between 'letting-go' and 'forgiveness'?" We had a lengthy conversation about this on the porch of my cabin, The Farmshed, and then later that afternoon, in the Refectory (where we cook and eat) while he and Aspen played Scrabble, I made this forgiveness life-cycle diagram in a flash.

I will discuss the idea of the life-cycle first, and then dive deeply into each point, in the clockwise order they are shown. The idea of a life-cycle of forgiveness was first presented to me by Don E. Stevens at the Young People's Group gathering number seven, which became the basis for the book *The Door-bell of Forgiveness*. At that time Don admitted to the gathering that while he did not know "the mechanics" of forgiveness, he knew we would find out. He emphatically charged us to do forgiveness work "in our own backyards" as he put it to us, meaning in our own lives and relationships, and then we would be authorized to share about forgiveness with others. At that time, I had never done forgiveness work anywhere, not in my backyard, or with anyone ever. I had no idea what the mechanics were, that is for certain. It wasn't until I started working on this with forgiving my father for his suicide, and then moving on to other personal relationships that extremely gradually this notion of mechanics or a life-cycle started to dawn.

Early on in the "Forgiveness with Meher Baba" seminars I started to see patterns emerge of what is required for forgiveness to flow, and I will attempt to share that below now, in the context of this diagram. I believe that one or all of these steps are needed, however the order may be different depending on the situation and how many people are involved. After making this diagram, I started composing a new set of diagrams (in my head) about forgiveness triangles, squares, pentagons, etc. based on how many people are involved in the situation and what their roles are, but that is another chapter.

My Forgiveness Life-Cycle has at least 10 stages, in this order (although some stages may be happening in parallel). This life-cycle assumes there are at least two people involved in the process, and there is giving forgiveness, asking for forgiveness, or both:

1. **Identify what happened.** In Non Violent Communication (NVC) terms this is the "Observation." While this stage may seem like common sense it can get more complex,

such as when a memory is repressed or only partial. In my work with people, I have seen that in the retelling of the incident, more than once, the details of the incident may in fact become more clear. The story may change from a dim memory of what happened to a clear and potent story with many more details and sometimes greater depth of injury than in earlier versions of the incident. Identification can be done in many ways, such as writing about the incident (e.g. the NVC Forgiveness form we created), or verbally, or through artwork like art therapy. Whatever medium of communication is best for the situation is fine, as long as the problem can be as clearly identified as possible.

2. **One of the benefits of the NVC approach is that Observations are separated from Feelings in the describing of an incident.** This is helpful on many levels, in that it can untangle the thread of mixed feelings, and memories of what happened, which if communicated all at once can be confusing. To move into only communication about the "feelings" associated with the incident is helpful. To be fair, some people have great difficulty describing emotions and feelings. This stage would benefit from a handy list of feelings as is easily found on many websites.

3. **Once the feelings are identified, it is important to fully** *feel* **the feelings.** Aspen said, "...allowing oneself to become immersed in the emotion is paramount." Again, this may seem to be obvious, or common sense, but I have found that many are resistant to feeling their own feelings

around a painful incident. This can lead to other problems, such as is found in psychological circles of splitting or fracturing of the psyche, or other "shadow" related issues. Since I am not psychiatrically trained, I won't go into that more here except to say that allowing oneself to feel the feelings associated with the incident will naturally lead to the next stage. In my own life, during my second forgiveness project from Baba, when I felt my feelings, they went so deep that I literally had a seizure and fell off my chair onto the floor while trying to express myself. I have never had a seizure before or since, but the pain of my emotions caused an electrical storm in my mind, I am certain. I hope this doesn't dissuade anyone, all I am saying is, that was a transformative day, and it did naturally lead to the next step for me in my life.

4. **Share what happened with someone safe.** It may be that we share directly with Baba (or God) within first, before involving another person. It is also possible that all these stages are done with a therapist, or in the absence of a therapist many people work on their issues with their circle of family and friends. So, in this stage, "someone safe" it means that it is important when sharing about the incident, and the associated feelings, you select someone who is safe. Safe is a relative term, and it means many things to different people, but because of the nature of trauma and forgiveness, it should be a trustworthy person who will not go around telling others what you are disclosing in confidence with them. Choose someone who will not judge you, and

someone who knows how to listen and honor your words, your experience and your feelings. If you have no one like that in your life, then it is recommend a therapist be invited into your process.

Aspen asked at this point, "Can God be that safe person? And, what if someone doesn't have the freedom to tell others?" Of course, throughout history God has always been present and available to all who reach out wholeheartedly and with love. And Meher Baba has and does play this role of being present and guiding those who love him. Baba said, "Remember me and I am with you, and my love will guide you."

In conversation with Jeff Wolverton on this point, Jeff said that in addition to being safe,

> Someone who can help you by keeping the feelings alive at the deepest level, for an extended period, so that they can be more fully experienced, is important. In other words, to help you face this issue, and facilitate you delving as deep as possible into those feelings. Even then the awareness will want to pull out of something that is uncomfortable. Bringing it before Baba, as if he is right here, is of course the safe place, and it invites him to be a part of the process. And in the healing process, he has infinitely more options on how to deal with forgiveness than we do.

Input from Annie and Jeff came at Meher Spiritual Center, March 2016.

As Annie Lovett shared with me, also on this point, "It is important to fully feel your feelings."

5. **Share what happened with the other person (or people) involved in the incident.** This is where the stages of forgiveness may get the most intense. There are many issues involved in sharing with the other person. This brings up the forgiveness directions, and the need for continued safety in your life and process. It is possible that you feel it is impossible to share your experience of what happened with the other person. It may be that the only way to share with them is through a third party, like a friend or mediator, or a therapist involved. During the seminar work we have done, I have repeatedly heard that an individual attempted to share, but there was no interest on the part of the other to listen. Another case is when the other is no longer reachable (they moved, or you lost contact), or they have since died before you were able to bring this issue up. In any case, we feel that while this stage can be vital and helpful it is not required. My own case, when forgiving my father for his suicide is a great example of this. In that case, I decided to share my forgiveness with my father at Meher Baba's Samadhi, since he had long since died and there was no question of what had happened. Many times, when sharing what happened, the other person involved may have great difficulty hearing about it, either interrupting, or becoming less than gracious in the listening. This is a natural

part of the process, and if it is too frightening, again involve a third party, or a safe mediator, or therapist.

6. **Acknowledge what happened.** Of all the things that seem to block forgiveness, the one that comes up the most in the forgiveness work I have done is the one wanting to forgive says about the person they are trying to forgive, "But they didn't even realize they have done anything wrong, and they don't agree with me!" In other words, there is a fundamental disconnect when, in attempting to forgive, there is no acknowledgment of the incident itself as needing forgiveness. When this happens, it can be a long and painful process of either waiting for that acknowledgment (which can take months or years in some cases), or just cutting to the chase: "Letting go."

I have found that the NVC process of writing out observations, feelings, needs and a request can discharge a lot of the pent-up emotions surrounding an incident, and pave the way for a more fruitful and healthy dialogue between two or more people. Emailing, or snail mailing such an NVC letter also has the benefit of allowing the recipient to review the issues before being thrust into an intense conversation. One might write such a letter, send it and then maybe a week later, follow up with, "Hey, did you have an opportunity to read that letter I sent you? It is important to me." Or something that allows the other person to enter into the process in their own time. Naturally with such charged material, it is ideal to have a facilitator, such as a therapist, but it is not always possible.

Another possibility is that this stage is surrendered as a "nice to have" but since it is not happening, working with all the other stages as fully as possible. In the case of my father's suicide, I never got any acknowledgment from him, other than what I wrote about in my chapter in *The Doorbell of Forgiveness,* which was a response I felt came from Meher Baba about my forgiving my father.

7. **Acknowledgment of feelings about what happened.** This stage is similar to the previous stage about acknowledgement of the incident itself, but it goes much deeper. If one cannot acknowledge what happened, it is almost impossible for the process to go deeper into the vulnerable place of sharing the feelings and emotions surrounding the incident. Once shared, naturally there is a desire to have the feelings acknowledged. As with the previous step, that acknowledgement may come, or it may not. We encourage the sharing of the feelings regardless of the response or result. This sharing of the feelings also can be in many forms, or mediums. It may be a written letter or email, or it may be verbally, or via some artistic medium like a song or a painting or drawing. Whatever communicates can be helpful.

I remember in Flagstaff, Arizona, there was a project where victims of sexual or physical abuse were invited to make a t-shirt design with colored paint and hang the t-shirt on a clothes line along other abuse t-shirts. I participated in this, and made a shirt. It was a powerful acknowledgement process for me indeed. Reading the other shirts alone was healing.

Aspen reminded me that another example of acknowledgment is the fabulous book, *Post-Secret*, in which individuals wrote extraordinary secrets anonymously. Frank Warren created *PostSecret* and invited anyone to simply mail him a secret on their homemade postcard. He received over a million postcards, and published the best of them. This response must be a reflection of the need for this acknowledgment step in the global psyche of humanity.

PostSecret: Extraordinary Confessions from Ordinary Lives, by Frank Warren (William Morrow, 2005).

8. **Giving Forgiveness or Receiving Forgiveness.** Depending on the people involved and the forgiveness directions, this can be complex, but this stage of giving and receiving forgiveness with love is the crux of the process, and it can be quite beautiful. There are as many shades and tones, and hues, and sounds related to this work as there are hearts, so no two forgiveness acts are ever the same. Let it be whatever it is without trying to compare it to anything else.

9. **Wholeheartedly Letting It Go.** This stage of letting go may not happen overnight, but what it means is that at some point you stop obsessing over it in your head, and you

wholeheartedly release it. It means – at least in part – to let go of wanting to punish someone (or oneself) for what happened in the past. Admittedly, this step can take days, months, or even years, depending on the situation. One indicator, in my experience, that it has been let go – is that it no longer pushes itself into your daily consciousness. It is as if it has receded, and left gentle peace after the raging storm. Naturally it can be remembered and brought back to awareness, but it no longer intrudes on daily thoughts.

Meher Baba emphasized this stage in the 1930s when he repeatedly told his Western Mandali (close disciples) and other followers that after a heated argument one should just let it go – release it. Here is an example from Baba's life, when two of his female disciples had been quarreling, and he directly intervened:

> Love and forget. This is the only thing that matters, and it pays. Almost all of you are weak. By weak, I mean taken up with desires. Anger is weakness, pride is weakness, and so on. If a mother found her child weak, she would love it all the more. So all love more. Don't you remember what I told you in Nasik? Learn to say, 'Janay-doe' [Let it go in Hindi]. Give up wanting the last word. Give up all wants and be happy. But you must try consciously. Now be happy. I forgive you all, but continue trying.[55]

10. **Being in the Present, Moving on in Freedom.** When I first created this diagam I was skeptical that there could really be ten stages to forgiveness, but the more I reflect on this diagram and write about it, the more certain I am there are probably more than these stages, and these are just the most obvious ones to me. The last stage is to live more in the present moment and move on from the past in freedom. This is harder than it appears, most likely because it is the nature of the ego to remain attached to past wrongs and hurts, but it is the nature of God and the angels to move on and heal.

Meher Baba said,

> Duality signifies separateness. Separateness implies fear. Fear causes worry.
>
> The way of Oneness is the way to happiness; the way of manyness is the way to worry. I am the One who has no second, so I am eternally happy. You are separate from your Self, so you always worry. To you, what you see is absolutely real; to me, it is absolutely false.
>
> I alone am real, and my will governs the cosmic illusion. It is the truth when I say that the waves do not roll and the leaves do not move without my will. The moment the intensity of your faith in my will reaches its height, you say goodbye to worry forever. Then all that you suffered and enjoyed in the past, together with all that you may

experience in the future, will be to you the most loving and spontaneous expression of my will; and nothing will ever be able to cause you worry again.

Live more and more in the Present, which is ever beautiful and stretches away beyond the limits of the past and the future.

If you must worry at all, let your only worry be how to remember me constantly. This is worthwhile worry because it will bring about the end of worry.

Think of me more and more, and all your worries will disappear into the nothing they really are. My will works out to awaken you to this. [56]

REFLECTIONS ON THIS LIFE-CYCLE

This is the life-cycle diagram I created for this project. As you read through this book, you will see other approaches that use some, but not all, of the same steps, or which have different steps completely. I invite you to think for a while and create a sample life-cycle of your own, which you can use as a starting reference point for your own work on forgiveness.

---

[54] *Listen, Humanity*, by Meher Baba, p. 73.

[55] *Lord Meher*, p.1922.

[56] Ibid, pp.4372 & 4373.

Chapter Twelve
Forgiveness and Intimacy

> I love you. Do not worry about your weaknesses.
> Eventually they will go. Even if they linger, love will
> one day consume them. Everything disappears
> in the Ocean of Love. – Meher Baba[57]

I RECENTLY HAD A GREAT CONVERSATION with my old friend, Marlena Applebaum ("Mar"), about forgiveness. We had worked together in the past, with Don Stevens, on the book *Sexuality on the Spiritual Path*[58] and other projects, including his Young People's Group (YPG). Mar has a deep mystical experience of life, and she is a trained psychologist, having earned a Master's Degree from Sofia University[59] (formerly the Institute of Transpersonal Psychology). Suffice it to say I value her profound insights – spiritual and psychological, and isn't forgiveness a little of both?

When I described what my experiences have been conducting the Forgiveness with Meher Baba seminars, she said I needed to add something to this book. I asked her to tell me what it was I had shared that struck her as important, to which she replied:

> Write what you told me about – how in your forgiveness groups the open authentic sharing greatly increased the

intimacy – between people who had known each other for years but never connected on that deeper level before...[60]

LAST MESSAGE ON THE ALPHABET BOARD

When I was explaining to Mar about how the intimacy we created in the seminar was so important, I spontaneously stated: "That is what *Meher Baba's Last Message on the Alphabet Board* is all about." In other words, at least one of the points of what Baba was conveying to me in this message, was that we form "internal links" with each other, which I am sure requires sharing, listening, and a level of intimacy. Here is the message from Baba in its entirety:

Baba gave this message on October 7, 1954.

There is no reason at all for any of you to worry. Baba was, Baba is, and Baba will also be eternally existent. Severance of external relations does not mean the termination of internal connections. It was only for establishing the internal connections that the external contacts have been maintained till now. The time has now come for being bound in the chain of internal connections. Hence external contact is no longer necessary.

It is possible to establish the internal link by obeying Baba's orders. I give you all My blessings for strengthening these internal links. I am always with you and I am not away from you. I was, am and will remain eternally with you, and it is for promoting this realization that I have severed external contact. This will enable all persons to realize Truth by being bound to each other with internal links.

Oh, My lovers! I love you all. It is only because of My love for My creation that I have descended on Earth. Let not your hearts be torn asunder by My declarations concerning the dropping of My body. On the contrary, accept My Divine Will cheerfully. You can never escape from Me. Even if you try to escape from Me, it is not possible to get rid of Me. Therefore have courage and be brave.

If you thus lose your heart, how will it be possible for you to fulfill the great task which I have entrusted to you? Be brave and spread My Message of Love far and wide to all quarters, in order to fulfill My Divine Will. Let the words `Baba, Baba' come forth from every nook and corner of the world and from the mouth of every child, and let their ignorance be reduced to ashes by the burning flame of My Love.

Come together in order to fulfill My Will by taking your stand on Truth, Love and Honesty, and be worthy of participating in My Task. I give you all My blessings for spreading My Message of Love.[61]

FEEDBACK FROM THE PARTICIPANTS

I have been contemplating the feedback we have received, over a few years now, regarding the forgiveness seminars. I would like to share some of that feedback and reflect on how sharing about forgiveness issues in a group setting, listening, opening our hearts, and then holding the space for intimacy allows for us to go deeper as a Meher Baba community. I selected three feedback excerpts, as I feel they are truly representative of the need for intimacy as we move forward in this "Post-Mandali Era" as some are now calling it:

> To me, the most remarkable thing about the workshop was the high degree of trust that participants showed one another. The result was a high degree of honest sharing and open vulnerability. That, in turn, led to expressions of caring and love seldom seen. Talking about forgiveness turned out to be a good vehicle for getting the group to come together... I was heartened by the level of loving and genuine communication among the people who came.
> – Billy

Billy was a highly interactive participant and deeply committed to the success of the Meher Baba community. I love what he shared with us, particularly when he said "the high degree of trust that participants showed one another" which led to honest sharing, and vulnerability. This seems like such a healthy recipe for the Meher Baba community (or any community) as we navigate this phase of our life-cycle.

I was so moved by it all. I have never participated in anything quite that deeply personal with this community, that turned out that connective and healing in the end. Good stuff. There really is something to this work that is in line with what Baba says about inner links of his lovers. I saw that so clearly this weekend... The main highlight for me was seeing, hearing and witnessing people opening more deeply to the group. Revealing truth and shame. So powerful in linking all our hearts and revealing each of our essences more. I haven't ever felt more connected on a heart level to this group. Really potent opportunities for us as a community.

     — Alisa

Alisa was not only highly interactive, but when I asked for a volunteer co-facilitator she immediately stepped up. I happen to know that Alisa has been a Baba lover for decades, so for her to say she had never "participated in anything quite that deeply personal with this community" struck me as a profound call to action, and confirmation that this work is spiritually important. This is real interpersonal work, and the results have been extremely encouraging. I am convinced that Baba is guiding me to continue this work with forgiveness, more and more.

We had a request, and then reached consensus as a group of 22 to split into three smaller groups for day two of the seminar.

For me it was not so much about forgiveness as it was about hearing others and being heard. Not so about forgiveness as Love. We began the meeting with a reminder

and demonstration that Baba's sign for Love and Forgiveness are the same. Baba would draw his hands, semi-
clenched as if holding something, up from his stomach,
and at chest high open his hands, push and release what
he was holding. 'You are forgiven, I love you.' I need
more of it and think we all would like and need more
Love and Forgiveness.

   – Harold

Harold is one of the most honest people I have ever met. He
gave much more feedback, but I believe the essence of it is the
creation of a more loving version of the Baba community in and
through forgiveness. One of my primary goals, in facilitating
this forgiveness work is to place everyone in a circle, facing
each other, looking into each other's eyes, listening to each
other's stories. This is a radical departure from us all facing
forward, sitting silently and listening to a Mandali member
speak into a microphone about what it was like to be with Baba.
It means listening to our spiritual sisters and brothers speak
about what it IS like to be with Baba right now. For even this
much of a shift, I am grateful. Going deeper from there, into
spiritual love and forgiveness, is the real thing.

[57] *Gift of Love*, by A. Dadachanji, p. v. (Beloved Books, 1996).

[58] *Sexuality on the Spiritual Path* (London: Companion Books, 2007).

[59] See: http://www.sofia.edu

[60] This description she wrote to me the next day Sept. 13, 2015 (12:16pm PST) in a Facebook chat message.

[61] *Practical Spirituality with Meher Baba*, by J. A. Grant, p. 216 (Merwan Pub.: 1987).

Chapter Thirteen
Toward a Forgiveness Geometry

The greatest virtue is called charity, not this ordinary
charity. Real charity means tolerance due to
big-heartedness. Tolerance and forgiveness are
included in real charity. It is also charity to
offer the other cheek when slapped. In fact,
to lose to make others gain is charity. It is a vast thing.
— MEHER BABA[62]

SHORTLY AFTER WRITING ABOUT the forgiveness life-cycle, I realized that the way I had been thinking of forgiveness was rather
two-dimensional, in that the "forgiveness directions" I had previously imagined, such as forgiving oneself, forgiving another,
asking forgiveness from another, asking forgiveness from God,
forgiving God, forgiving a group, and asking forgiveness from a
group, were basically what I was working with. Then I had a
sudden inspiration to look at forgiveness in terms of geometry.
This is meant to be a tool that may help someone who has difficulty determining what exactly is going on in any given situation, to clearly understand who is involved, and what needs to
happen to restore health.

We will give you sample images for you to work with. When
you make your own diagrams, just fill in the names for each

point, and draw the arrows whenever you discover a valid for-giveness direction. Try to label the arrows with any words about what needs to happen in that relationship to restore health and peace and beauty (or Oneness). This is an exercise in forgive-ness directions beyond the two dimensions:

1. Forgiveness as a point = forgiveness of oneself. This may mean asking forgiveness from yourself, or forgiving oneself or both. Whatever the process is, it is personal and individ-ual and wondrous – just trust it, and don't worry whether you are "doing it right."

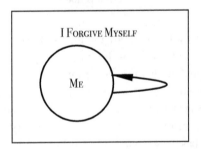

2. Forgiveness as a line = forgiving another, or asking for-giveness from another or both.

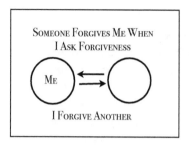

3. Forgiveness triangle = forgiveness working out between three people, and naturally this is more complex. For example a husband may declare: "I am having trouble forgiving Martin for how he just treated my wife Brenda, and I need to process this." In this case, the husband (let's call him Ken) has a problem. A person he knows has done something to his wife, and now the three of them have a forgiveness triangle to deal with.

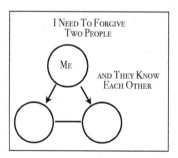

4. Forgiveness square, or diamond, or pyramid with three corners (if 3 dimensional helps). In this case there are four individuals involved in the situation. Let's say it is two married couples, and they went away together on a vacation and things melted down badly. It doesn't matter why, what matters is they are suffering and stuck, and by the time they reach home, there is a forgiveness issue (or many issues) looming among the four of them. Use the image of a square or a diamond or a pyramid that has three corners at the base, to help diagram the situation. We offer the pyramid only if it helps illustrate the relationships or problems, if not go back to the diamond or square.

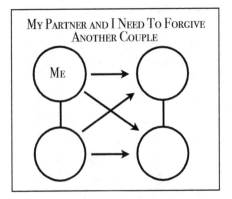

5. Forgiveness pentagon, or pyramid with four corners at the base. This is the complex situation where there are five people involved in a forgiveness drama of some type. Only use the pyramid (3D) structure diagram if it helps illustrate the nature of the relationships, otherwise use the 2D pentagon, which is flattened.

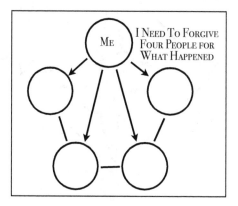

6. Forgiveness hexagon, or a double-pyramidal structure (two four-cornered pyramids with bases touching), also an eight-sided die in gaming. This is obviously a very complex situation, and use the hexagon structure to map the relationships and the directions of what needs to transpire for forgiveness to come into the picture. It is okay if there is no arrow going between some of the six individuals, just do

your best to show what is going on in the situation. Later we can apply forgiveness where it is needed.

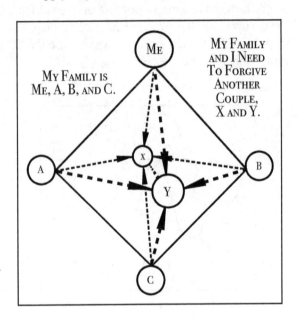

Two more shapes:

A. Let's imagine a cone shape, for the relationship between an individual and a group. In this case, an individual is asking forgiveness from a group, or an individual is forgiving a group. Or, a group is asking forgiveness from an individual, or a group is forgiving an individual. In any case, the cone shape is a great representation of this. Think of the point of the cone as the individual and the round cone base as the group.

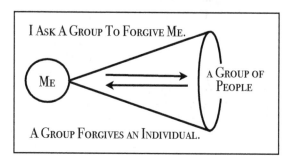

B. Let's imagine a cylinder shape, to represent two groups working to forgive. What the details of this are can be worked with in the forgiveness worksheet, but label the two ends of the cylinder with the two group names, and the edge of the cylinder (between the two ends) with the nature of the problem and what needs to happen.

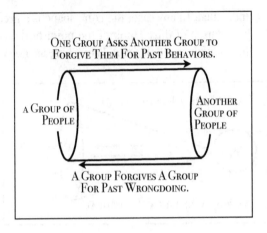

This can go on forever, naturally, but the point is to map out using geometric shapes (of any kind) whatever you see (and feel) about all the people involved. Use arrows to indicate the forgiveness directions – where love needs to flow. You get the idea. While working on a diagram, if you realize there are more people involved, upgrade to a larger shape! Be bold and daring and just put it all out there and look at it. The purpose of this is to gain awareness of the issues, and the formations of the relationships, and needs around forgiveness.

Now that you have created your own forgiveness geometry diagram, go to the chapter on the NVC Forgiveness Worksheet, and apply it to the diagram you have just created. If that works, try it again with another situation, and another shape.

---

[62] *Lord Meher* (online edition) p. 4149.

Chapter Fourteen
It is the Same

DURING A RECENT Forgiveness with Meher Baba seminar, in Myrtle Beach, South Carolina on October 10, 2015, I gave the participants some "forgiveness exercises" to complete. It is an original worksheet, giving directions about four basic steps, and modeled after the Compassionate Communication work of Marshall Rosenberg. This has proven to be an extremely effective seminar tool. After the exercise, we gave the group the opportunity for some to share their experience of processing their forgiveness and – if that participant wished – to also receive feedback from the group.

One of the participants, Brian Walsh, had this to share:

> After doing your exercise, I realized that – I need to forgive myself. Then, contemplating it more deeply, I realized –
> I need to ask God to forgive me. Finally, I realized –
> it is the same.

I was stunned by this simple truth, and I filled with joy when he shared this with the group. After the seminar I looked for him, and found him in the living room of our host's home. I told him how incredible his sharing was, to me. He seemed shy, and didn't think it was that fascinating. I assured him it was a mystical truth.

By truth, I don't mean to imply that the ego-self (or "small-s-self" as some call it) is identical with God. But I don't believe that is what Brian was getting at with his comment. In contemplating all of this, I was reminded that in his seminal writing, some of which was turned into a small book titled *In God's Hand*, Meher Baba himself showed this relationship between God and Self ("big-S-Self"). That book contains some of the only writing we have from Meher Baba which is literally in his handwriting (thus the book title).

Because we can see Baba's actual handwriting, we can also discover something fascinating. While it has been many years since I reviewed those pages, I remember vividly one page, because of the tremendous impact it made upon me. The page had a sentence in which Baba was writing about "God," and he crossed out the word God with one strong stroke, and changed the word to "Self." I had an intuitive knowing when I read that sentence over and over, that Baba was doing much more than writing, with that alteration. He was in fact teaching the world a giant lesson, with eight strokes. In this new advent, and what he named The New Humanity, the old-world notions of God are being replaced by new mystical understanding and experience of God within as the Real Self.[63]

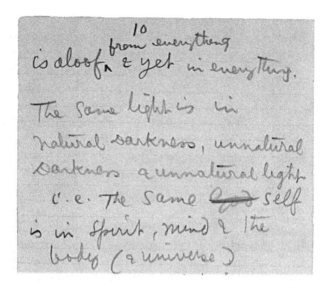

The edited sentence from Meher Baba's writing as scanned *In God's Hand* reads: **"The same light is in natural sanskaras, unnatural Darkness & unnatural light. i.e. The same ~~God~~ self is in the spirit, mind & the body (& universe.)"**

Later in his life, Meher Baba said "The only **Real Existence** is that of the One and only God Who is the Self in every (finite) self." And further, he expounded on this difference between the false limited self (ego), and the Unlimited Real Self, in his *Discourses*, "The Nature of the Ego and its Termination":

When the ego gradually adjusts itself to the spiritual requirements of life through the cultivation of humanity, self-lessness and love, whole-hearted surrender and offering oneself to the Master as truth, it suffers a drastic curtailment. It not only offers less and less resistance to spiritual unfoldment, but also undergoes a radical transformation. This eventually turns out to be so great that in the end the ego, as an affirmation of separateness, completely disappears and is substituted by the Truth which knows no separateness. The intermediate steps of slimming down the ego and softening its nature are comparable to the trimming and pruning of the branches of a wild and mighty tree, while the final step of annihilation of the ego amounts to the complete uprooting of this tree. *When the ego disappears entirely there arises knowledge of the true Self. Thus the long journey of the soul consists in developing from animal consciousness the explicit self-consciousness as a limited "I," then in transcending the state of the limited "I" through the medium of the Master. At this stage the soul is initiated into the consciousness of the supreme and Real Self as an everlasting and infinite "I am" in which there is no separateness, and which includes all existence.*[64]

Discourses, "The Seven Realities," Volume 1, p. 15

Ultimately, I feel Brian has landed on a mystical truth. When we can truly know and forgive our self, it is the same as God forgiving us. This is profoundly true for me.

---

[63] *In God's Hand*, by Meher Baba at Avatar Meher Baba Trust web site: https://www.ambppct.org/Book_Files/IGH_%201.pdf (accessed 2/14/2016).

Within the PDF it is p. 25, but it is the handwritten page with Baba's page number 10 at the top. The published book is: *In God's Hand: Explanations of Spirituality in Meher Baba's Own Hand*, by Meher Baba (New Jersey: Beloved Books, 2000)

[64] *Discourses*, by Meher Baba online: http://discoursesbymeherbaba.org/v2-82.php (accessed Dec. 26, 2015).

Chapter Fifteen
Forgiveness and Harmony: Giving In

D<small>URING</small> S<small>EPTEMBER</small> 2015, after a deep discussion on forgiveness over the phone, and with my encouragement, Vanessa sent me this email which started to capture her feelings and thoughts about "Forgiveness and Harmony," as she put it:

from: Vanessa Weichberger
to: laurent@ompoint.com
date: Thu, Sep 17, 2015 at 8:13 AM
subject: Forgiveness and Harmony - giving in

Forgiveness and Harmony. Baba's oneness is reflected in the harmonious exchange amongst all of His beings no matter their differences. There is a chapter on "Harmony" from *The Real Treasure*, by Rustom Falahati, wherein he speaks about giving in to create harmony. [65] It is a conversation between Rustom and Eruch:

> {Rustom to Eruch}: Shouldn't such a person be stopped in what ever way he should be stopped? Eruch shook his head, "That would be your weakness if you resorted to such a means."
>
> Then what should I one do? I asked
>
> "Give in," Eruch replied without hesitation. "For the sake of harmony let him have his way. Harmony is more important than anything."

Forgiveness supports the divine plan of love and harmony God is. Forgiveness allows for the many of us who are in all stages of growth to experience love and their own path to realizing the truth within themselves.

> Eruch continued: "So, from the point of view of the God-realized soul every soul is bound in falseness of illusion. Remember there is no such thing as right or wrong."[66]

In terms of abuse, every person has a right to have a healthy, balanced life. In other words, abuse is not something one has to accept to "create harmony" or to "give in." One can defend themselves (see the *Discourses* on defending one's self or others or country), walk away or choose another path to avoid the conflict or abuse. Justice is a form of love. Perhaps Baba has something in his discourses on justice, karma etc.?

Love, Vanessa

---

[65] *The Real Treasure*, p. 41.

[66] Ibid, p. 42.

PART II
Contributing Authors

Chapter Sixteen
When Meher Baba
Asked for Forgiveness

by Amrit Irani
San Gemini, Italy 2018

In this chapter, we interview Ms. Amrit Irani as she graciously tells the story of when Avatar Meher Baba himself once asked for forgiveness. This was narrated to us by Amrit in San Gemini, Italy on April 23 2018, and transcribed by Laurent from an audio recording (which he made with her permission). We have lightly edited the transcript for clarity, grammar and punctuation. We use curly braces {...} for describing what's happening in during the interview. Present at that time of storytelling in Italy were Amrit Irani, Vanessa & Laurent Weichberger, and Nick Principe. It should be noted here that one of the last things Avatar Meher Baba did publicly was to perform the marriage ceremony of Amrit to Dara Irani, at Meherazad India (in the Fall of 1968). Dara is Baba's nephew. Baba was extremely pleased with their marriage.

Let's listen to her story now:

Amrit: It all happened in 1949, 1950 and 1951 in the New Life:

So, this is the time, the New Life time, when Baba was in north India, and my family had just been introduced to Baba. That's another story of how they got introduced to Baba. My father had offered food, and Baba asked, "Would you send the food regularly to us?" And because Baba didn't stay in New Life Cottage, and near my folks, where the cottage was built for him, he was something like seven or eight miles away – more inner side of the city of Dehra Duhn.

My father said, "Yes Baba." So Naja talked to my father and said, "The food you are sending is just delicious." Simple food, rice and daals and vegetables and all that. "But for Baba, cook separate rice every day, more softer."

We like our rice to be firmer but Baba liked the softer rice, it was easier for him to digest, and plain daal. On one of these occasions we were talking about – my father didn't have a car, he had a motorbike, and with the help of a servant boy my mother would pack all the food and Baba's rice, there in one of the smaller bowls, and tie it up, with a sheet, and he will hold it between himself and my father and they will take it to Baba. One day she forgot to send His rice. When my father went there, Naja came running out saying, "Baba hasn't eaten anything, and I don't see Baba's rice. What happened?"

My father said, "Huh?" And he realized his wife forgot. He got very annoyed with his wife, who was at home, not there.

Laurent: And his wife is your mother.

Amrit: My mother.

Laurent: That's your father and your mother.

Amrit: Parents. My parents, Kumar and his wife.

Laurent: What is your mother's name?

Amrit: Subhadra.

Laurent: Subhadra? Like Krishna's sister!

Amrit: Krishna's sister. Baba said to her, "You are my sister." So, actually this daal which she used to make for Baba, Baba named it "Subhadra's daal."

Vanessa: Wow!

Amrit: So often they used to make that in Meherazad until many, many years later. Subhadra's daal, today. Anyway, so, my father got very annoyed, and so Naja realized that he is very unhappy. She must have told Baba, or they came to know that Kumar was very annoyed with his wife for forgetting. So, Kumar came back home, and must have shouted at his wife, or whatever. I wasn't born that time.

Laurent: This is before you were born?

Amrit: Just while my mother was pregnant with me, at that time.

Laurent: You were in your mother's tummy while all this was happening?

Amrit: While this was happening, during the New Life. I am a New Life baby, yeah.

Laurent: Wow, okay.

Amrit: So, my father told mother that – you know, "How could you forget Baba's rice?!" And all this thing, you know? So my mother (I don't know 100% the words, but she was annoyed herself), and she must have said, "What's the big deal, I forgot?" Do you know?

So, he got very angry and he slapped her.

And as soon as it happened, within half an hour or so, one of His very close Mandali (and I think it was Keki Desai – who was travelling around with Baba, from Delhi, during this New Life time), was in Dehra Duhn with Baba. On a bicycle he followed Kumar home, and came home, and said:

"Baba sends a message: 'Don't be angry with your wife.'"

But my father says, "Sorry, it is too late."
{Amrit starts chuckling to herself.}

Laurent: Too late.

Amrit: He came half an hour later, you know, it's already happened. And then that person went back, and said to Baba: "By the time I got there Kumar was very angry, and his wife argued, and he slapped her..." Because they must have told Him the whole story. Time passed by. Father used to go every day with the food, and Baba told my father, "Never ever do that again, for any reason, raise your hand on your wife like that." So they thought the story was over.

Then Baba came to a place called Meher Marfi, which is my family home. And Baba's cottage was built there, with a well and all that, and Baba was coming there. And without announcing (my mother says she wasn't even ready, usually they are always ready whenever they went for Baba) – she was in her house working, and Baba comes – and straight to her, and stands there with folded hands, and said, "Please forgive me, Subadra, because of me your husband had punished you, your husband was angry and slapped you."

My mother said she was shaking with tears pouring out, and then He gave her a big hug. And then he said, to Kumar, "In front of me please you ask – you say sorry too."

Laurent: Meaning to, "...say sorry to your wife"

Amrit: To his wife. So, my father said sorry to her too, publicly and with other people there. And of course, after that we –

that's another thing you see? I have never seen my father raising his voice to his wife. Not only that, he always called her Subhadra-ji. "Ji" is for the respect, like Bhau-ji, etc. {Suddenly in the background can be heard old Italian church bells which start ringing loudly nearby.}

Amrit: Bells are ringing. Baba says, "When bell is ringing, it must have happened."

Laurent: Right.

Amrit: He always called her Subhadraji.

Nick: So, Baba changed their entire life!

Amrit: Entire life. A whole family's life. He sowed that respect and with that there was so much love. Respect alone is not enough.

Note: While transcribing I heard the word, "sowed," as in sowing a seed in soil, but then again, it could have been "showed" which she spoke. Both words will work in this context. I wrote to Amrit in India, via email, asking her to please review this transcript but she did not respond, so we leave it to the reader to decide." – L.W.

Laurent: Jai Baba!

Amrit: Jai Baba.

Chapter Seventeen
The Road to NVC

by Vanessa Weichberger
North Carolina, 2018

NVC is Non-violent Communication as described by Marshall Rosenburg in his seminal book, and has the format:
1. Observation, 2. Feeling, 3. Need, 4. Request.[1]

Please allow me to briefly describe who I am, and my background. I grew up in California and New Mexico, very much exposed to the Meher Baba communities in both locations, and they became my extended family in many ways. I was an artist who devoted myself to painting and drawing Meher Baba's image. From the age of nineteen, I embarked upon many trips to Meher Baba's Samadhi (tomb) at Meherabad, India and embraced sincerely my spiritual path throughout my life. During the early stages of having my own family, we moved to Myrtle Beach to be ever nearer to Meher Baba's presence and love at his universal spiritual center in South Carolina. I endeavored to listen to God's direction through my heart, and intuition, so when the opportunity came into my life to put NVC and forgiveness into action, I was thrilled and hopeful. I was excited to see how this could be used, and to see the shift it would make in my life. I had been trying to find ways to communicate in a healthier way on my own, and was definitely not finding the results I was looking for, so much so that I wondered if just "keeping a vow of silence" would have been more effective than anything else I had tried. I was ripe for a new communication option when NVC came along and gave me a way to put Meher Baba's words into practical action in my life.

This is my experience implementing Non-violent Communication in my life. I was first introduced to NVC long ago, about ten years ago, and never followed up. I never felt drawn to learn it even though I was in a relationship which had destructive communication. The power of having a coach bring it to the table, in this case Laurent, was key for me in accepting this communication style.

When NVC returned to my life, I was in the process of getting divorced, and I was in such a state that it took me six months to really be able to sit down and write one NVC letter with clarity and confidence on my own. It sounds ridiculous to me now, but I was overcoming years of old communication patterns and so I had to address and really look at my thoughts. I had to sift out my judgements from feelings, and distill what was most important for me to focus on. Sometimes I came to the realization that I really had two (or even three) NVC letters to write since I had more than a couple of needs and requests related to a single experience which I had. In short Laurent had to do a lot of hand holding to get me from Point A to Point B. During this time I read out loud numerous of my NVC letters to him in the process of learning the method before I would send them.

On this journey I found that distilling my own communication down to its simplest form not only helped me better grasp my own thoughts and needs but also helped the receiver understand what is being communicated. The receiver was able to understand so much better and faster what I, the sender, was sharing. As time went on, the NVC letters I wrote during the divorce process rarely received a response. However, the development of my understanding of myself and the awareness I was gaining was phenomenal. A response was not required for my growth.

Soon I was putting NVC to work in my relationship with Laurent as well. As we know, our romantic relationships can be sticky to address since they involve our most-inner feelings and experiences. I found I had to train myself to use NVC in all areas of my life. Even then, as I would start writing an email my old patterns would creep in – specifically criticism and accusatory judgements. When I was deeply triggered about a specific experience which happened between myself and Laurent, I found that in the worst of mental states NVC was still possible. It was actually an incredible tool to help dig me out of an emotional rut. I could wake up at 3:00 am (processing and obsessing over an interaction we had), write out my NVC, and have such an emotional release that I could go to back to sleep easily.

Now, when I hand out the "golden NVC formula," I watch as many are fascinated and interested, however rarely do they reach the implementation stage. If they manage to write an NVC, once or twice, rarely does it become a part of their regular healthy communication and things slip back to the old communication patterns. I think this is in part due to the momentum of their past sanskaras keeping them bound in their old habit patterns, but also NVC really addresses deep fears of not "being seen," of not "being heard," and of experiencing rejection or humiliation. NVC also is a surrender.

We are all in a type of addiction to our anger and fear.

When anger or fear comes into play, the normal forms of protection a person has developed are employed. These forms of protection the ego might manifest appear in many ways. We see them as power struggles, unrealistic expectations, putting each other down,insulting behavior, fear of being fired, and fear of looking weak or incompetent. How can anyone navigate all of this in a healthy way?. Everyone must be courageous enough to keep the NVC process going by taking each day at a time.

As Laurent once pointed out to me, having to face a true "No," or a true "Yes," or a final "No," is also very confronting. It ends the drama and creates such a clarity that a problem (or issue) can truly be left behind. I think, looking back at my adoption of NVC and now witnessing years of Laurent educating many with it, the coaching process was key for me and for others. Having an NVC mentor is a fabulous way to really get the NVC ball rolling and having it become a regular practice, especially if the other parties involved are not communicating using NVC. In fact, most people are not using NVC and this brings added challenges to embracing this process.

NVC by its definition of function brings all parties up to a new standard of operating and essentially creates a whole new atmosphere of light and love, and true understanding. It cannot be overstated how much psychological work all parties involved could be doing since essentially, they would be creating a new paradigm of understanding.

Fear is a common theme when people realize they must deliver their newfound direct communication to a person (or group) whom they must face or work with daily. Over time, I have found myself walking my thoughts through the NVC process when faced with challenging circumstances in the moment where I knew I needed to verbalize a boundary, or my need promptly. With the strength developed from all my writing of NVC letters I have ventured to verbally implement it, which can be a bit of a challenge since you don't want to accidentally stray from the formula and go down a rabbit hole. For this reason, I still use the written form as my go-to NVC form, so that I can collect my thoughts and create a healthy rapport.

I am years in to using NVC and I still face my fears and baggage when faced with delivering it. - VW

In conclusion, NVC is a real and solid solution for the establishment and preservation of healthy communication. The single greatest NVC challenge is in the commitment of the people in implementing it. As in my relationship with Laurent, he plays the role of keeping himself and myself accountable for using NVC and not falling off the track. In that light, having a person who plays this role in a business environment would also be invaluable.

NVC paves a path to forgiveness through mutual and conscious understanding and communication. Once a person has shared their observations, feelings, needs, and request(s) in the NVC format the ability for the receiving party to understand just exactly what that person is asking for, and is feeling, frees a person to respond specifically to the request. It halts the back and forth of the typical confusing statements, off point statements, misunderstandings, and general toxic communication styles, which often create further damage. I have found I was better able to see my part in the matter, and the other person's point of view, thus paving the way for real forgiveness. It is infinitely easier to ask for forgiveness, or to forgive, when a person can see exactly how the other person is feeling, what they need, and how they are experiencing a situation.

In Baba's love.

----

1. *Nonviolent Communication: A Language of Compassion*, by M. Rosenburg (Encinitas: Puddledancer Press,1999)

Chapter Eighteen
My Forgiveness Journey

by Shu-Yi Hsu
New York, 2018

Forgiveness in Chinese is Yuanliang ("原諒").

In Chinese, it means, "Original assumption/ thinking." It can also be translated as, "Original understanding."

The following forgiveness journey I am going to share is my attempt to understand why my marriage broke down. It is the story of how I started a journey of forgiveness to reconcile the conflicts with my ex-husband and myself. But, before that, I am going to share a story of who I am and why I came to America.

原 yuan

諒 liàng

forgive

Background
I came to New York City to pursue my graduate studies in 2012. I wanted to advance my education in a masters program, however, I was horrible at taking written exams, which were the major filtering process to get into graduate schools in Taiwan. I attempted four times in six years, and I still didn't get accepted

into any schools. As you could imagine, I was extremely frustrated.

I was teaching Mandarin as a second language to foreign students for these six years. One day, my student, Shane, asked me why I wanted to teach. I explained my educational philosophy – I would like to make my students fall in love with learning Mandarin. I wished to help them develop to a functional level of Chinese. I wanted my students to be life-long Chinese learners.

After hearing this, Shane paused for a second and suggested that I consider applying to graduate programs in the United States. He offered to help me with the school applications and test preparation. I was very excited, however I also hesitated to take the offer. I didn't have the luxury to pursue graduate school overseas because of the of financial burden involved.

MY FAMILY

My Dad was a helpless optimistic gambler regardless of how many times he failed. I loved him, and I hated him, because he has repeatedly hurt the family by putting us in a never ending cycle of debt – not to mention that he was never home to take care of the family.

During the year when I was preparing my school applications, my family was undergoing turmoil again. Two consecutive debts hit us through Dad's reckless investments. I was furious, and I asked my Mom to divorce him. She refused because she was afraid of living a divorced life. She insisted on staying in the marriage. Because of her decision, I decided to take the opportunity Shane offered and focused on graduation school applications.

MY BLESSING AND BETRAYAL

After one year of hard work, I finally had a fruitful result. I was accepted into not one, but four graduate schools! On the other hand, it was a heart wrenching decision to tell my family that I would take this chance to study abroad. Most of my family and friends were confused about my decision. The entire family was almost broken because of the debt my father had accrued. My parents were facing foreclosure on their house, and had no place to live. Additionally, the cost of graduate school was so high that most of my loved ones did not understand how such an education would be of value.

Hakka or Hakka Chinese refers to Han Chinese who speak a dialect, Hakka. The Hakka-speaking provinces are Guandong, Fujian, Jiangxi, Hunan, Zhejiang, Hainan and Guizhou. In Taiwan, Hakka Chinese accounts for about 13 % of Taiwanese population.

Furthermore, growing up in a "Hakka" family, women are discriminated against culturally. Women are not considered equal to men in traditional families. Investing money for women to pursue higher education is considered "wasteful-thinking." So, perceived as a betrayer, I left the family in dismay, and fear of financial crisis, to pursue my personal career development.

MARRIAGE AND GRADUATE STUDENT LIFE

Studying at graduate school was challenging because I had a hard time reading, as English is my second language, and that also negatively impacted my writing. The constant struggle of academic work, and the limited financial resources put me in a great deal of stress. Looking back, my life was full of challenges, fears and uncertainties. Additionally, I felt very lonely in such a big city like New York. I was single for over six years, and naturally I was longing for a romantic relationship.

Paul and I met in 2013 summer. One day I saw a grad school girl, who was out on a date. I asked her where she met her date. She told me they met using online dating. I was not convinced of the idea of meeting people online, but I decided to give it a try. I created a profile and dated a few "matches," but it wasn't going anywhere. I went to a friend and told her that my online dating was not satisfying. She replied that it is a "numbers game," meaning the more you date the better odds you will have... so I gave it another try. Shortly afterwards, I met Paul. He was the last person I dated before the fall semester started.

Paul was twelve years older than me, and born and raised in New Jersey. There were many differences between us and we seemed to be in totally different leagues. We continued to date. I was attracted to Paul because of his personal characteristics. He is one of the most empathic people I know. He is kind and generous, and he helped me to understand a lot of social and cultural nuances in American society.

For example, Paul would always pause a TV show if I had questions about a specific word, or the cultural connotation in the conversation. He also helped me to identify salient sexual and racial discrimination present in everyday life. He trained me to be more assertive as a woman, and educated me that I shouldn't tolerate being treated as less because of my female gender.

We lived together for a couple of months before we decided to get married. I was depressed and had no money. I made the marriage leap because I felt if Paul could love me unconditionally, even seeing my worst. I could choose him as my life partner. I proposed to Paul, and then we got married in 2014.

MARRIAGE BREAKDOWN

During the first two years of our marriage, Paul was undergoing a career change. He wanted to become a website programmer so we sent him to a "coding boot camp." However, he had a hard time picking up the new skills, and his frustration caused him serious depression which was hard for me to discern at that time, because I did not know him over a long period of time. During this transition period, I was the main bread-winner of our household. We had an extremely high overhead of household bills that we could barely meet. That was one of the main reasons that caused our marriage to break down.

Then suddenly, I was out of my job in the summer of 2015, and I was so scared. I felt helpless, angry, and frustrated because we didn't have any financial cushion or support network. I started to lose faith in our marriage, and I told Paul I didn't admire him anymore because he couldn't take care of the family when I needed him to.

Later in the winter of 2015, I had an accident when I was hiking in the mountains. I fell from a rock and broke my three front teeth. Back home, Paul was still struggling to find a job. Without any income and the expected dental bills from my accident, I didn't know how I could continue my life in the U.S.A. My dental trauma, the household financial stress, and our marriage crisis put my life on halt. I was depressed. I started losing my hair and losing weight. I felt my life was completely out of control.

How I met Laurent

I met Laurent because we used to work in the same software company. He is always friendly, and carries a big smile. He coached me in Big Data, and generously provided help when I reached out. Once in a while, I would ask him what he did in his free time. He would talk about his art work, and his publications centering around Meher Baba.

Initially, I wanted to show appreciation of Laurent's support so I purchased his book, Forgiveness with Meher Baba. After reading the book, I immediately fell in love with it. I was in awe of each protagonist's story in the "Contributing Authors" section, and their courage to transform their struggles into love, and into the forgiveness journey.

Attending the Forgiveness Workshop

After we both left that company, I still connected with Laurent once in a while for life and career advice. When Laurent told me that he was going to facilitate a "Forgiveness with Meher Baba" workshop in San Francisco during April of 2106, I told him that I wanted to attend. At that time, I was trying to put my life back together. I felt the forgiveness workshop could help me release my resentment and frustration towards my husband, Paul.

The workshop was taking place in an artsy and cozy house. During the next two days, we sat in the living room with a fireplace and a lot of antiques, and piles of old albums. There were about eight of us seated in a circle, and we shared our stories, and we each chose one person whom we felt deeply that we needed to forgive.

I explained that my purpose in attending the workshop was to reconcile the conflict of my broken marriage. I wanted to forgive my husband (as we were still married at that time), and forgive myself for all the suffering we had undergone.

Opening up myself

Initially, even as I was sitting in a workshop, I was not ready to share my story. I had too much resentment, and I had a hard time finding the motivation to forgive Paul. Fortunately, Laurent created a warm and safe environment during the workshop. Through everyone's talking, I gradually opened up and let my emotion out. At that time, I felt failing in my marriage was shameful. I did not want to describe Paul as an irresponsible husband, because he did take care of me in one aspect, however, he failed me in another aspect. I also blamed myself for failing to support him with his career transition.

During the workshop, I was trying to recover the original understanding of Paul's unsuccessful attempts at finding a job. He tried, but ultimately failed many times. I saw him suffer and I also suffered. He was a really nice man, a loving and supportive partner, my mentor, and also my therapist. He gave me words to understand and maneuver myself professionally and academically through difficult conversations. I felt full of shame that I could find no motivation to support him like I used to.

This forgiveness journey is not only about reconciling the conflict with Paul, but with myself.

I was disappointed that I couldn't stick to our wedding vows, and wanted to give up on the marriage. At the time when I went to the workshop, I already lived separately from Paul, because of my work needs. I avoided the conflict, and pretended I was fine. I thought that I had stopped the bleeding, but I never dared to examine how badly I was wounded. I was very glad that the forgiveness workshop gave me enough courage to commence the journey of forgiveness. The process of healing is still going on today.

How I met Rick Chapman

The day we finished the forgiveness workshop, I was told by Laurent that he had an important date with his friend Rick Chapman right after the workshop. Laurent invited me to join them. We drove to a nice town of Oakland, and sat in a gourmet café. While we were waiting for Rick to arrive, Laurent gave me some background information about him. As a young scholar back in the '60s, Rick traveled to India to meet Meher Baba, and he is one of the only people still alive who has had personal contact with Baba.

I immediately knew Rick was highly esteemed, and it was a special and honorable opportunity to have this meeting.

Rick appeared with a long trench coat, a hat, and an umbrella. He is a tall and slim gentleman, boasting a big white mustache. His eyes were shining, and he talked loudly, and laughed loudly. He and Laurent were throwing jokes back and forth. I remembered I described Rick and Laurent both as very "sassy." I explained that I was drawn to learn more about Meher Baba because I am very attracted to both Laurent and Rick's characteristics – witty, warm, caring, calm, and loving. That is, loving to the people who are wounded and need to be helped. I was incredibly lucky to have such a private and intimate moment, and I know that I was loved and supported.

I ended the journey full of love and blessings. I was given three books about Meher Baba, and a bookmark that says, "Be Happy." Rick asked me to share my reflections about the book with him. I remember together we walked Rick back to the parking lot. He was driving an old classic vehicle. I didn't know if there would ever be a chance to see Rick again, but that's definitely a once in a lifetime experience.

Later, I also exchanged a few emails with Rick. I reached out to him when I was undergoing some conflicts, and stressed from academic life. Rick always gave me lots of blessings and encouragement. I was very grateful that I felt supported and loved by Rick, even though we only met for an hour. I felt we were connected because we were both practicing Meher Baba's discipline, to love.

POST-FORGIVENESS WORKSHOP AND THE START OF MY SPIRITUAL JOURNEY

In 2018, Paul and I decided to get divorced and I moved from our New Jersey home to New York City. One of the hardest things about leaving him was knowing that I would be alone again, by myself in such big city. This fear caused me to have anxiety and panic attacks. To fight against my anxiety, and build my support network, I started searching for spiritual belonging. I started attending church, community groups, and Bible study.

In addition, I also became extremely attached to my mother. I called her on the phone almost every day, for a couple months, and I was constantly upset that I couldn't be with my family. I tried to get Mom to visit me, but she refused. She said she didn't have any desire to travel. It really hurt me. I was craving her love, and I really wanted to be close to her. Instead, I felt like an abandoned child. I was angry at my Mom and frustrated.

One day, Laurent reached out to me to check on me. I shared with him my conflict with my Mom. During the conversation, I attempted to understand my mother's rejection, and her thinking process. Suddenly, I realized the conflict I have had with my mother was not about – how she didn't want to travel to the U.S.A. To her, coming to the U.S.A. and not being able to speak English scared her. She also didn't want to add any financial costs for me. She worried about me. I started to realize that this conflict is not a behavioral issue, but simply emotion and fear.

By understanding the reasons which caused my mom's refusal to travel, it allowed me to forgive her. I needed to forgive her for not wanting to see her own child. I also know that to resolve this conflict, I had to tackle her fears as well. This perspective helped me to learn I was not deserted, I was loved. This is my ongoing forgiveness journey. I can foresee more conflicts, but I also feel courageous and empowered to resolve conflicts, and being able to forgive others through practicing learning the "original cause," and thinking behind people's actions.

Chapter Nineteen
Forgiveness

by Jennifer Tinsman
Myrtle Beach, South Carolina (October 2015)[67]

DEAR FORGIVENESS BROTHERS AND SISTERS,

I wanted to share a simple, yet powerful, little paragraph about forgiveness I found in, of all places, a Jehovah's Witness monthly handout and how I came about receiving it.

Have any of you seen the movie *The War Room*? It is a wonderful movie about a sweet, elderly black woman who teaches a younger woman how to handle her life struggles through prayer - in what she calls her War Room - a special place she has created for prayer in her clothes closet. It is a great movie if you are so inclined. The character in the movie touched Paul's and my heart.

Around the time we saw the movie, a very sweet black lady with a younger companion showed up at my door. Although they made it clear they were Jehovah's Witness the lady reminded me so much of the lady in the War Room that I could not resist and invited them in. She is sweeter than sweet with a heart you cannot resist and takes her work for the Lord very seriously. We have developed a relationship now and she comes every month bearing a big smile as she sits among all of the Baba photos in my living room and shares.

I made a conscious decision to open my heart to this woman, and to forgive my religious prejudice against her chosen faith, to welcome her as Baba would, with nothing but a smile to match hers and to listen when she speaks, as she listens when I speak. I am grateful to Baba for this experience of reaching beyond my limited perceptions to touch, and be touched, by a woman who although of different Faith, exudes an authentic love for God and the ability to spew pearls of wisdom if I can shut up long enough to hear her.

Frankly, like most people, I usually take the handout she gives me and promptly recycle it but this month I decided to see how they did things in her world. I was delighted to see this small write up on Forgiveness since, like you, I have been making a conscious effort to better understand the subject of forgiveness and put more effort into making it a daily practice in my life.

Here is the paragraph:

Forgive Freely
What does it mean? In the Bible, sin is likened to debt and forgiveness is compared to the cancellation of a debt. (Luke 11:4). One reference work says that in the Scriptures the Greek word translated, "forgive" means to let go (of) a debt, by not demanding it." Thus, when we choose to forgive someone who has wronged us, we let go of any need for reparations from the offender. Our

willingness to forgive does not mean that we approve of the wrong behavior or minimize the hurt that it has caused us. Rather, we simply decide to let go of resentment, even though we may have a legitimate "cause for complaint."

I love this wonderful description of forgiveness and I must admit that it makes me feel very powerful and joyful to be able to say to someone, "I am not demanding repayment for your mistake" (or spiritual ignorance), and how freeing this feels.

Thank you for the opportunity to share my forgiveness journey with you.

With Love and Gratitude,
Jennifer

---

[67] This was originally sent as an email to the group which attended the two "Forgiveness with Meher Baba" seminars we conducted at her and Paul DiStefano's home in Myrtle Beach during 2015.

Chapter Twenty
Stepping Into Loving
and Letting Go

by Alistair Cockburn
November 2015

I was jealous of John from the beginning, he was clearly the person who had always been popular in high school, the center of social activities. I had always been the outsider. It was the same in our three-month-long class on leadership. He drew others toward him, and I felt like the outsider, again.

A year later, in a class on communications where John happened to be assisting, I sat at the end of a row, looking for a partner for the opening exercise. John slid into the seat next to me. I turned to him and said, "I have to tell you, I had a chip on my shoulder against you all through that class. You reminded me of the guy who was always popular in high school, and I never was. I watched you through all those months, and could never bring myself to come and talk to you, I was feeling so wound up about it."

He said, "I have to tell you, I had a chip on my shoulder against you all through that class, too. You are so freaking smart, you reminded me of the brainiacs in my high school I could never talk to. I watched you through all those months, and could never bring myself to come and make friends with you."

Something happened at that moment. We each dropped our barriers toward each other. I felt a channel of love, palpable and nearly visible to me. It was a tube, the width of our bodies and connecting us at the stomach and chest. I nearly vibrated from the sensation. We stared at each other for five, ten, I don't know how many seconds - clearly he was feeling what I was feeling. We were connected by unadulterated love. The room faded away, we had only sensation of love for each other for this period.

It went away, the room came back, and we sat staring at each other in shock, with nothing to say. I might have said something like, "I just felt total love for you," and he might have said something back. I don't know, we were so rocked by what had just happened. We gave each other a warm hug as the exercise closed, and he went back to his position assisting the class.

This was not an experience of "forgiveness" as I had ever heard it described. There was no act of contrition, no repentance, no benediction, no permission to continue. There was simply love, with no space for any other thought or sensation.

That unique event in my life is in sharp contrast to my usual approach to forgiveness, which is unilaterally lowering the negative energy of an event to zero, in order that it does not block my future. Robert Brault sums it up:

> Life becomes easier when you learn to accept an apology you never got.

I call this "evaporating energy."

I have practiced unilateral forgiveness, or energy evaporation techniques, for years. Here are five that I will describe:

1. Anchor new associations over the top of the old ones.

This comes from neuro-linguistic programming , or NLP. See http://www.nlpu.com/Articles /artic28.htm

2. Concretely imagine a different future to step into.

This comes from the solutions focus school of psychotherapy, where you concretely imagine a different future, identify what is already working in that direction, and accentuate that. See http://sfwork.com/inbetween-neither-inside-nor-outside

3. "Accidentally forget," through meditation or another method.

4. Set a timer and just quietly watch the energy evaporate over time.

5. Reframe the event so there was never any fault to forgive.

Each of these, except the last, is based on the observation that you can't erase a memory. Once it is there, it stays there. Worse, remembering a memory replays it, which makes it stronger. Therefore, working through old memories does the opposite of what we want, which is to make the old associations weaker.

We cause new associations to take priority over the older ones instead, letting the old ones become weaker over time.

Before going farther, it is important for me to say that I am not a licensed psychologist or psychotherapist, nor a trained

NLP practitioner. I am only an engineer who reads a lot and has all-too-many negative moments to get rid of, er, forgive, so that I can get on with the good things in my life.

WHAT IS FORGIVENESS, ANYWAY?

I need to start by contrasting this thinking with what many people consider to be forgiveness:

"Display contrition, and earn redemption."

That is the sort of forgiveness we so often see adults teaching children:

"Johnny, say you're sorry."
        "I'm sorry." (mumbled)
"Billy, now forgive Johnny."
        "I forgive you." (mumbled)
"There, now go play."

I suspect that this use of the word has a Christian origin, where, starting from original sin and divine forgiveness, we wishfully mix those concepts into our daily lives, as though the forgiver has the power to offer redemption to the other. This interpretation not only is wrong in many ways, as I will get into later, it also causes much distress.

Given my younger indoctrination into that use of the word, I was really surprised to find the following dictionary definition of forgiveness:

"to stop feeling anger toward (someone who has done something wrong)"[68]

This is basically energy evaporation, with the exception that it still adds in the concept of wrongdoing. Here are the first four techniques:

TECHNIQUE 1: ANCHORING

Imagine you see a person, "Pat," walking down the street wearing orange shoes. You were badly offended at an early age by a person, who – all you remember – was wearing orange shoes. You feel emotions piling on you from earlier days, but you have been working on forgiveness and you decide that it is time to apply the discussion-contrition-redemption approach.

You walk up to Pat and start a dialogue about your experiences and feelings and your need to forgive ...

Wait – what?

Here is Pat, walking down the street, and this very energetic person comes up and starts talking about this earlier trauma from someone who once wore clothes the same color, insisting on a dialog about hurt feelings and need to forgive. Pat goes, "What? What do I have to do with all of that? Why are you dumping on me?"

In this scenario, you dumped a load of negative energy on the unsuspecting Pat. Even if you are so lucky as to walk away feeling that you have forgiven the original offender (and Pat alongside), you have transferred negative energy to an innocent person, who now has to deal with that.

In contrast, imagine that instead of talking about your early trauma, you walk up to Pat and say, "Really nice orange shoes you have there!"

Pat is likely to look up in surprise, feel positive energy coming from you, utter something like, "Thank you," and continue walking along feeling a bit happier than before.

You not only just changed Pat's life for the better, you changed your own, by creating a new and happy association with orange shoes.

Your goal is not to erase the old, painful memories, but over time, to make them irrelevant. By adding new positive associations with orange shoes, you strengthen them until they become your primary association.

The first few times I tried this, I felt cheated. I had been looking forward to the release of anger, the recognition of my pain from the other person, the recognition of my worth as the other person apologized, and the warmth of being able to forgive the other person.

I didn't get any of those.

Instead, the association to the negative thing simply weakened and generally disappeared. No "justice" was delivered to me, there was no contrition, no redemption. I just went about my new life with one less weight on me.

I have to say that this new sensation took some time to get used to.

Now I look forward to it. It is kind of fun to watch with how little effort the mind can replace something having so much negative energy with something else positive. It is as though I took off tight shoes and can wiggle my toes again.

TECHNIQUE 2: DESIGN A FUTURE TO STEP INTO

The hypnotherapist Milton Ericsson did not name his use of this technique in the 1950s and 1960s. In the 1970s, De Shazer and Berg constructed it as a deliberate approach, calling it Solutions Focus. You will want to get one of the books to learn it properly. Here, however, are its four basic steps:

1. Imagine your future as it will be when the problem is no longer there. Describe that future situation aloud, clearly, concretely, in intricate detail.

2. Describe what other people will notice in you that indicates to them that you are in this good state. Describe how they will act toward you, so that you can tell that the problem is no longer with you.

3. Look for all the things that are already in your behaviors now that match what you just listed.

4. Start using and amplifying those behaviors, so they occupy more of your attention and your time.

When I got divorced, my ex did some things I considered unspeakably bad. At that time, I could not possibly have sat down and had a discussion about how I felt and how she felt. (Actually, I did try once, and she said, "I have too much anger right now, let's just talk about how to make the future work." So much for me feeling like the offended party!)

I chose to imagine her as two people, the one I had loved and with whom I had spent many pleasant years, and this other person, whom I didn't know at all. Then I could at least think about this first person, talk about her and our wonderful shared time together.

I imagined her in the future, being happy in her new life, our grudges being old enough as to no longer be relevant. Whenever I thought of her, I tried to see her becoming that happy person. This was actually distressingly easy to do. I knew what she really wanted in her life, and it was easy to see her achieving that. And, in fact, she has. She has actually stepped into the future I imagined for her (and I'm fairly sure she imagined for herself). We met at our son's wedding, and although we were not in the state of unadulterated love as I described in the opening story, we were able at least to greet each other on open, friendly terms and proceed through the day.

Visualizing a concrete future has been useful for other things, such as reducing fears. I used it once to get comfortable with talking to my boss:

I used to tremble when talking to her. So I visualized myself sitting there comfortably, and used the mantra "I am relaxed and confident when talking with her." I visualized and repeated before each visit to her, and found that after some months, I really was relaxed and confident when talking with her.

While that example is not about forgiveness, it does show the technique in use.

Technique 3: Meditation and Accidental Forgetfulness

Transcendental Meditation is a very simple meditation form. All you do is repeat one syllable over and over again for 20 minutes. "Om" makes a good syllable, although I was given another one in my introduction.

When I meditated after being annoyed by someone, I found that I "woke up" without that annoyance in my head. It had somehow disappeared.

As with re-anchoring, I felt cheated of a good mad. There I had been feeling some offense, and was bathing in the warm glow of righteousness. But the heat of anger and the warm glow of righteousness had quietly been taken away from me during the meditation.

Having wondered about this for years, I offer a small explanation of what happens. During meditation, the uncontrollable mind starts a train of thought. At the moment of remembering to say "Om," the brain terminates that train of thought and puts it away somewhere. After some number of repetitions of putting things away, the brain finds a tidy home for the train of thought, considers it dealt with, and goes onto whatever next thought is carrying energy. By the time the meditation is over, the brain has processed the emotions around the event, and there is nothing left.

I call this "accidental forgetfulness."

It may not sound or look like forgiveness in any of the usual descriptions, but it definitely reduces negative energy, it fits the dictionary definition of forgiveness, and therefore goes into our toolkit.

Walking the 20-30 minutes home from work each day had the same effect. As I walked, I replayed negative events from the day. When I finally opened the door to the house, it was with a pleasant, neutral energy, as the negative events had all been dealt with, much as from my meditations. I think the mechanism is much the same. (And as an important note, driving a car does not have at all the same effect, because the brain doesn't have the free capacity to do all the processing while driving).

These rapid energy-evaporating techniques have an odd side effect: the other person might feel cheated that you resolved the issue without interaction!

Imagine that you finish your meditation or your walk home. Twenty minutes have passed. The phone rings. On the other end of the line you hear, "I just wanted to call and apologize. I feel so badly. Will you forgive me?"

And you say, "Whatever are you talking about? Huh? That? Oh, I've already forgotten that."

Now your interlocutor feels cheated of a good catharsis of redemption.

Technique 4: Set a Timer

When I worked in a research center, I had a boss who destroyed the careers of several of my colleagues through her (bad) guidance. She came close to doing the same to mine. I fought her for seven years, and when I finally left, I had a lot of negative energy in my thoughts around her.

After a few years, I decided that this negative energy was getting in my way, and I needed to get rid of it.

I noticed that my negative thoughts were already weaker than they had been a few years before. I wondered:

"How long it will take before this negative energy is gone, and those events don't carry any more energy for me?"

And I set a time marker.

Every so often, maybe each year, but I didn't make a ritual about it, I checked my energy level around her and those years, and was happy to see them diminish. I didn't worry or fuss about it, I simply trusted that time would weaken those memories and associations, as I filled my life with new ones.

It took about five years. Now, while I have not "forgiven" her, in the sense of feeling any particular love for her, I find no particular emotional charge in thinking about her. She is just a person again.

I had a similar experience some years later, when I was on sabbatical in Norway with my family.

My boss loaded me so heavily that year with really critical assignments that I neither had my sabbatical, nor saw Norway, nor indeed saw my family much. I was extremely angry by the end of the year.

About a year later, I set that timer again. It took some years for the energy to evaporate. Although I have not forgiven him in the more interesting sense described in this book, the events are so remote by now that I hardly notice one way or another. I am alive, I have a good life, those things happened as though to someone else, and I have no particular energy around them.

I once combined both the NLP visualization and the timer idea:

After my divorce, I was unhappy, even in fear, for several years, as the lawsuits dragged on. At one point, perhaps when the end was in sight and the worst was past, I had this thought:

"I shouldn't still be unhappy. Look at me – I am walking down the street, peacefully, in good health. I have money in the bank, the weather is fine, and no one is actually stabbing me at this moment."

I visualized a numeric scale going from -10 to +10. I would mark my state as negative if I was actively unhappy or in pain, and positive otherwise. I reserved +10 for being in the middle of the best sex ever, and worked down from there.

Walking down the street, I decided that I was up to at least +4, since there was nothing wrong, and I was enjoying the walk down the street. I wasn't in a good conversation, or dancing, but it was generally good.

In my visualization, I noticed that the marker on the scale was a pleasant green color, but that there was this "echo" or trail of red markings to the left of it, running down to about +1. It seemed that my body was telling me that although it was technically at +4 at that instant, it carried remnants of more negative states.

I ran that visualization often over the next months. I paid special attention to when it moved up (anchoring the positive associations). I noticed as it went to +6, then +8 or even +9 when I was, dancing, with friends, or in particularly good conversations. Nowadays, it is rarely below +6.

After I found I was in a good state most of the time, I turned my attention to those red echoes, and wondered whether they would ever shrink.

Sure enough, they started to shrink, until one day I noticed the scale was a nice green +6, and had no red trail to the left. I concluded that my body had finally decided that the present had caught up with the past and it had no need to carry around warning signs from the past. The energy around my divorce had gone roughly to zero.

I got to test this some while later, when my son got married, and I had to meet my ex-wife for the first time since the divorce, five years earlier. We met, gave each other a bit of a nervous kiss on the cheek, she introduced me to her new husband, and we continued with the day.

Reflection: "Forgiveness" is Not a Word

It dawned on me, while writing the above, that "forgiveness" has a problem, as a word. It is not a thing to be done, because it is a negation of a negation, an absence of an absence.

"Forgiveness" contains some image of correcting a wrong, as though there were ever a wrong in the first place. But the idea of a wrong implies an authority for judgment, which is not present in many of the conditions we are considering. And a wrong, being locked in the past, cannot be corrected, any more than broken glass can be restored to its pre-broken state.

"Forgiving" is therefore trying to do something impossible: undoing something that never existed. I consider it a non-word, a collection of letters that we carry around by habit and try to find a meaning for. That is one reason it is so frustrating to us.

Oddly, this idea leads me to technique #5: Reframe the past, so there never was any wrong to correct.

TECHNIQUE 5: REFRAME THE PAST

The mind is a funny thing. We cannot erase a memory, but with just one new piece of information, we can reinterpret the past so that it feels entirely different. Here is an example:

You spend hours waiting for someone. They don't show up. You become livid. What an insult! You imagine all the things you are going to say to them, or perhaps decide you will never have anything to do with them again. What an apology they will have to make!

The next day, the person says, "I'm sorry I missed the appointment. My mother was in a car accident, and I spent the night with her in the emergency room."

In an instant, your indignation vanishes. More likely, you become embarrassed about your anger. There is no need for the person to apologize at all. The question of forgiveness is moot.

That is an extreme but not unrealistic example of reframing. With the new information, there is no longer any wrong to right, and so the idea of forgiveness becomes irrelevant.

What a beautifully simple way to lower the energy to zero – simply arrange in your mind that there was never any wrong in the first place.

It is easiest when we already know there is nothing to forgive:

A friend phones you at 9 p.m. The next day, he or she apologizes, "Forgive me for calling you so late."

You reply, "No forgiveness needed, it was a fine time to call."

See how easy that was? The friend raised the energy a little bit, and with your answer, you lowered it back to zero.

If only we could do that deliberately.

We can. Simply understand the other person.

When we understand someone else, we see their actions through their eyes and their value system, where their actions are reasonable and make sense. Seeing the world through their eyes and value system removes the sense of "wrong." There is nothing to forgive.

I never felt a sense of outrage when my wife asked for a divorce. I was also told that she had been having an affair, but neither the affair nor the request for a divorce generated in me a sense of being wronged. I understood the world both from her perspective and from a neutral viewer's perspective. Since she had not "wronged" me, in my view, there was nothing to forgive.

There are two obstacles to reaching this level of understanding.

The first is to recognize that if you succeed, your entitlement to an apology will go away.

The second obstacle is that you need to do the work well, to understand the world from the other person's perspective, so that the sensation of "wrong" goes away.

However, both of those are mostly a question of being willing to "not have been wronged in the first place."

STEP INTO LOVE OR LET GO.

Let us roll this discussion back up and see what we have.

"Forgiveness" is about undoing something that never was. In this sense it is a non-word, just a collection of letters hanging around us. However, there is still a real and negative energy level we feel toward a person and an event that we have to deal with.

The first and best remedy is to reframe the event so that there was never a "wrong" in the first place. Then there is no need to forgive.

Should that not be possible, for whatever reason, there are several techniques for unilaterally lowering your own negative energy around the event:

- anchor new, positive associations;
- create a different, positive future;
- "accidentally forget," through activity or meditation;
- set a timer and just let the energy dissipate over time.

Reducing the negative energy around an event is a useful thing to do, and in many cases you can do it all on your own. It does not actually rehabilitate the relationship with the other person, but it allows you to move on with your own life.

The final alternative is generating love, as in the opening story. Love is not about declaring a wrong and a right, of correcting a wrong, or of asking whether any person has been rehabilitated. Love simply makes all of those questions irrelevant. When the sense of love is in place, there is no space for the concept of wrong and right and judgment. The other person is simply welcome.

When I saw Meher Baba's dictum: "Love and forget. This is the only thing that matters," I originally saw a two-step process: love, then forget. However, reflecting on what I have written above, I see the forgetting as unnecessary. With love, there is nothing to forget, there is simply no room for anything else.

If you can't love to that extent, you can at least let go.

---

68 http://www.merriam-webster.com/dictionary/forgive

Chapter Twenty-One
Forgiveness and Trauma

A therapist's perspective on
neurological impediments to forgiveness

by Randall Overdorff
Gainesville, Georgia (September 2015)

Efforts to forgive may be hampered due to neurological impressions made by wounds experienced in the past. If the fight-or-flight response continues to be triggered from cues related to the wounds, or exposure to the perpetrator of the wounds, there are therapies available to help remove these obstacles to forgiveness.

Many people seek therapy due to traumatic experiences. Common to these experiences are fear and helplessness that trigger neurological fight/flight/freeze responses. Also triggered are shame and negative ideas that get bound to the memories, e.g. "It is my fault; I should have done something; I am a bad person." Wounds requiring forgiveness are perpetrated by others and also include an element of betrayal. Some examples of wounding experiences are sexual abuse, neglect from narcissistic or addicted parents, and physical abuse or verbal abuse by parents or significant others.

Often the offense remains a secret. If disclosed, others may minimize the offense. The victim may be blamed. The offender may deny culpability. He may be dead or far away. He may be a dangerous character that must be avoided. Such circumstances increase the difficulty of healing and empowerment.

Premature expectation that a victim forgive the perpetrator of an offense may serve to wound the victim once again. Families may press the victim to "just get over it and move on." The perpetrator may demand forgiveness, saying, "I apologized, so now put it behind you." Or the victim may be pressed to forgive on the basis of some spiritual authority.

Forgiveness must be freely given. Sometimes different kinds of giving can be highlighted in therapy. Codependent giving comes from guilt, shame, fear, a need for control. Such giving is exhausting and binding. A gift from the heart is freely given. It is light, liberating. Likewise, forgiveness increases bindings when it comes from shame or in response to coercion.

A victim can only freely offer forgiveness from a place of safety and empowerment. There must be an assurance of substantial boundaries for safety and confidence in an ability to be protected from additional wounds. Such prerequisites are often not available, for example when there has been no public disclosure of sexual abuse, and the victim must grow up with continued exposure to the perpetrator. Or when the victim of domestic violence continues to be in danger of re-offense by her partner. The presumption from others that the victim must forgive can be toxic. Adjuring the victim to turn the other cheek, when she continues to be slapped again and again, serves to diminish the humanity of the victim. Continuing in a relationship with an unrepentant perpetrator continues to wound the victim. Prior to forgiveness some public reckoning about the facts of the offense is necessary. Genuine repentance on the part of the perpetrator, including a willingness to provide substantial restitution, is also needed. Then the victim may have the basic requirements needed to choose to work toward a healthy relationship with the offender.

When the victim has forgiven, or "moved on," the offender no longer looms large in their consciousness; they are free of emotional triggers and negative cognitions related to the memory.

Even when the victim is in a stage of life when she believes she is empowered, sincere efforts to forgive may be blocked by continued vulnerability to triggers related to the offense. If not healed, the neurological impressions from the offense, when triggered, may cause the victim fear and elicit a shameful, helpless ego state similar to that experienced at the time of the offense. Also is elicited negative and irrational self-talk, for example, "I am worthless."

When struggling to forgive, obstacles may include continued obsession with thoughts of the offense or the offender. Memories, nightmares, or cues in the environment may continue to trigger disturbing fight/flight/freeze responses. These signal that the neurological impressions stemming from the offense remain unchanged. These symptoms are akin to those of people diagnosed with PTSD. Meditation, prayer, seeking spiritual guidance and intervention may provide release. If not, there are currently promising methods of psychotherapy that can help provide release from the neurological bindings of trauma, among them EMDR (Eye Movement Desensitization and Re-processing) therapy.

CASE STUDY

A woman sought therapy after becoming obsessed with her husband's infidelity. The affair happened over a year before. Her husband had apologized to her, resumed faithfulness, said he realized that he wanted his wife only, but refused to partici-pate in marital therapy. He was working hard, behaving well, showing contrition and attentiveness in his own way. She con-tinued to love him and her heart and faith inspired her to pre-serve the marriage. In therapy she increased her confidence and ability to assert herself in the relationship. She wanted to for-give him and move on. However, her obsession with his past behavior continued with the image of the other woman intrud-ing continually in her mind. Such images triggered fear, a sense of vulnerability and helplessness, and anger, with a desire to punish her husband that led to intense arguments.

Despite her desire to forgive, she could not because she con-tinued to be wounded by a replay of the neurological impres-sions formed by the injury of the infidelity. It was like the injury was happening again and again in the present. EMDR therapy helped diminish the emotional power of the memories, freeing her from intense triggers and frequent thoughts of the infidel-ity. The wounding events were placed firmly in the past, still important of course, but taking on a reduced emotional charge and meaning more in perspective with her current life and mar-riage as a whole.

Chapter Twenty-Two
Wounds, Healing and the
Path of Forgiveness

by Joe DiSabatino
Myrtle Beach, South Carolina (December 2015)

Forgiveness is an attribute of God – in Islam, two of the ninety-nine Names of Allah that pertain to this quality are *"Ar Rahim"* – "the Merciful One," and *"Al-'Afuww"* – "the Forgiver." When we forgive someone or ourselves, we are embodying in our own limited way this divine trait. Since the Infinite cannot be harmed in the slightest way by an action from a limited being, the Infinite is free to endlessly forgive because any harm incurred always falls on the one asking for forgiveness.

I have found it useful to work with forgiveness within the Sufi four layers of the heart model. The four layers are: the self/ego, the heart, the soul, the secret. How we respond to wounds that have been inflicted upon us or that we have inflicted on others will depend on the layer of the heart that we are living in.

All of us have been wounded and all of us have inflicted wounds on others. In the 1996 film *Independence Day*, actor Will Smith engages in an aerial dogfight with an alien spacecraft. He shoots it down, lands his fighter jet, pulls the alien from his craft, and punches him in the mouth with the greeting,

"Welcome to planet earth!" For many brand new humans, this is often the kind of reception they receive in childhood from their caretakers and peers.

Yet children have a natural healing mechanism when hurt physically or emotionally—they seek out a caring, safe person, usually the mother or mother-figure, and then they discharge their pain or fright by crying or getting angry or both. If the adult can act as a safe, loving, non-interfering "container" for the child's emotional discharge, then usually it is cleared out in the present without any residual effects. But how many of us had parents who were God-realized beings, always capable of giving us the kind of unconditional love we required in the moment? What frequently happens is that a child gets wounded a second time by the response given to his distress by an adult. His discharge process is cut short. So eventually the child has little choice but to shut down emotionally and develop ego-based coping mechanisms as a least-worst alternative to the natural healing process.

Coping mechanisms are survival tools, powerful opinions that serve as mostly unconscious guiding beliefs about our self, other people, and the world. Coping mechanisms are the voices of the self/ego whispering to the unconscious: "Given that such and such bad things are happening to me, then ... (fill in the blanks):

"I don't deserve to be loved"
"I have to conceal who I really am"
"I can't trust men"
"I can't trust women"

"I'm not smart enough"
"I'm not creative"
"I have nothing to say"
"Nobody cares what I have to say"
"People only care about themselves"
"God doesn't listen when I ask Him for help."

If you look at the content of most limiting beliefs based on coping mechanisms, they'll be seen to be twisted distortions of the ninety-nine Divine Qualities latent in our soul. For instance, instead of "I am a holy child of God who carries Divine Love in my heart," you might get a coping mechanism programming the heart to believe "I am a worthless alien who deserves to be whacked."

> The ego attempts to solve its inner conflicts through false valuation and wrong choice. It is characteristic of the ego that it takes all that is unimportant as important and all that is important as unimportant. Ego attempts to solve conflicts through false valuation. Thus power, fame, worldly attainments and accomplishments are really unimportant, but the ego takes delight in these possessions and clings to them as 'mine.' On the other hand, true spirituality is all-important for the soul, but the ego looks upon it as unimportant. - Meher Baba[69]

LAYER I OF THE HEART, the self/ego, even under optimal environmental conditions, veils us from the Truth of who we really are. But a wounded ego brings out its worst side, what the Sufis call the "nafs." A wounded ego taken over by a coping mechanism wants to build fortresses for protection, it retreats, collapses, denies, punishes, blames, counterattacks directly or engages in passive-aggressive sneak attacks. It doesn't ever want to forgive and it tries hard to forget but without real success. We create a humanity that is completely separated from the Reality of who we are. This victim stance can go on for a lifetime for some, or well into one's twenties or thirties for most.

Unhealed wounds imprinted into the layer of the ego/self in childhood are like running a finger through wet cement—there's a visible permanent scar created as the personality solidifies. They are stored energetically in our bodies and in our hearts.

> Love has to spring spontaneously from within; it is in no way amenable to any form of inner or outer force. Love and coercion can never go together; but while love cannot be forced upon anyone, it can be awakened through love itself. Love is essentially self-communicative; those who do not have it catch it from those who have it. Those who receive love from others cannot be its recipients without giving a response that, in itself, is the nature of love. True love is unconquerable and irresistible. It goes on gathering power and spreading itself until eventually it transforms everyone it touches. Humanity will attain a new mode of being and life through the free and unhampered interplay of pure love from heart to heart. - Meher Baba[70]

Many people are having spiritual awakenings these days and the infusion of divine energy often leads them to revisit their emotional wounds and their stance towards the people who have wounded them. It is a monumental shift in consciousness to go from living a life entirely from the ego/self to a heart-inspired life of love and service. If you are in pain or running from pain then it's pretty hard to not just forget but to permanently erase wounding experiences from your body, heart, mind, and soul. As people connect to the second layer of their heart, that place deep in the chest where we can begin to experience the Love and Light of the Divine, and start to face their wounds lodged in their hearts through some kind of therapeutic healing journey, they usually will feel a desire to let go of their hurt and resentment, to understand, contain, heal and discharge it.

They realize they are paying a huge spiritual price for not confronting their wounds, their shadow side, and that it's a win-win situation to forgive those who have hurt us in the past or to ask forgiveness from those we have wronged. There are many therapeutic methods for facilitating heart-based forgiveness such as psychodrama, directly engaging one's perpetrator in dialogue, writing letters to the perpetrator and not mailing them, reconnecting to one's wounded inner child, all the various modalities of body-oriented or verbal therapy, etc. Unhealed wounds in the heart are black holes that absorb Love and Light and drain our positive energy. Healing those dark places makes the heart a stronger and more integrated container capable of holding greater amounts of Divine Love and Light for longer periods of time.

In the second layer of the heart, forgiveness of others and ourselves becomes an essential spiritual practice in our journey home. We want to liberate ourselves from karmic bindings, to release our soul from having to spend time in some future lifetime being on the receiving end of a debt someone needs to pay back to us or vice-versa. We both have better things to do. The Sufis call this sincere heartfelt forgiving and plea for forgiveness *"Tawba."* We turn away from the world and try to wash our slate clean. Only Divine Love can do this. In Islam, the prayer *"Astaghfirallah al azim"* is an essential practice and means "Allah, please forgive me for my sins." Likewise, Meher Baba placed great importance on reciting the "Prayer of Repentance" that he dictated.

But even at this more advanced position regarding forgiveness, the person in Layer 2 of the heart still operates from the assumption that he/she was/is the victim, was/is unfairly treated. Now the response has changed to "You hurt me but I am willing to let go of my pain and forgive you of all debt towards me. I send you sincere love and well-wishes." Love has loosened up the frozen scar tissue in the heart. Remember the famous 1970s Vietnam war photo of a 12 year-old girl running naked down a road screaming from napalm burns? She was in the news recently. Now in her 50s, her back and legs are severely scarred. Recently, she started receiving laser light treatment that for the first time is starting to heal the old scars. Likewise, Divine Love is the Laser Light beam that can do the same to our emotional scars. It's never too late to heal them.

In the second layer of the heart, wounding experiences are like a finger passing through water. They create waves but the water soon resolves back to a state of tranquility no matter how intense the storm.

> The Soul is and always remains indivisible. The one indivisible Soul is the base of the different ego-minds which do the thinking and acting of various types, and which go through innumerable types of dual experiences; but the one indivisible Soul is and always remains beyond all thinking and doing and beyond all dual experience. Different opinion or different ways of thinking do not introduce multiplicity within the one indivisible Soul for the simple reason that there are no opinions or any ways of thinking within the Soul. The activity of thinking and conclusions drawn are within the ego-mind, which is finite. The soul does not think; it is only the ego-mind which thinks. - Meher Baba[71]

LAYER 3 OF THE HEART is the soul. A soul-based perspective is the Divine's viewpoint on our humanity and our wounds, not our own more limited perspective which characterizes Layers 1 and 2. The best soul-based forgiveness model that I know of is called Ho'oponopono. Joe Vitale's book "*Zero Limits*" (2008) made this Hawaiian healing model and Dr. Hew Len, Ho'oponopono's leading practitioner, an international sensation.

The Ho'oponopono method is meant to wash away memories, especially painful memories stored in our subconscious, so we can eventually return to conscious union with the Divine. Ho'oponopono starts with the premise that everything we experience on the outside comes from us, is a present or past-life memory projected onto the screen of our consciousness and then the outer world. Rather than believing in the truth of our projected memories, Ho'oponopono views them as yet another opportunity to wash them once and for all from the slate of our consciousness. This is totally consistent with Meher Baba's teachings regarding the formation and function of sanskaras.

> ...impressions are deposits of previous experience and become the most important factors in determining the course of present and future experiences.

Embracing the Ho'oponopono approach requires a radical shift in consciousness as one moves from Layer 2 of the heart to Layer 3 of the soul, a shift as profound and radical as moving from Layer 1 of the ego/self to Layer 2 of the Heart, as explained above. In Layer 2, there is still duality, still the conviction that someone out there wronged you, even if now you desire to magnanimously forgive him or her. You are still in the victim role. In Layer 3 of the soul, while using the Ho'oponopono method, one assumes 100% responsibility for every experience that comes into one's life, including being wounded, unfairly treated, etc. even though common sense says you were/are obviously innocent. In other words, this hurtful person has come into your life to remind you to ask the Lord for forgiveness for the same or similar hurtful behaviors you once did in the past.

One assumes 100% responsibility—without guilt or any self-blame-- because it is based on a deep spiritual truth. At Layer 3 of the Soul you are always on your knees inwardly, asking for forgiveness rather than giving it which is what you did at Layer 2. The Ho'oponopono basic practice is a simple four-step prayer that is repeated inwardly:

1. Please forgive me. 2. I'm sorry. 3. I love you. 4. Thank you.

This prayer covers all the spiritual bases and tends to make God's ears perk up with interest—taking full responsibility, repentance, love, gratitude. You can elaborate on each element:

1. "Please forgive me for any time in this life or past lives when I have done the same thing or something similar to what (name of person) did/is doing to me." "Please forgive me for any time in the past when I have lost my temper and become insulting and verbally abusive," etc.

2. "I'm sorry, I will never do that again."

3. "I love you"—love is directed to the Divine, to the other person who appears to have hurt you, or even to your own memory/sanskaras that created the wounding experience. The important thing is to try to feel love in your heart.

4. "Thank you"—for this golden opportunity to wash clean a painful memory that had been stuck in my subconscious for perhaps lifetimes.

I can think of two caveats regarding Ho'oponopono. If someone is stuck in blaming or the victim state, it's best not to be a

Ho'oponopono preacher. Ho'oponopono is for your own clearing of memories, a tool to help you return to Source. If you are listening to someone stuck at Layer 1 of blaming or even Layer 2 of "I forgive you" and you can see what they are doing 'wrong,' or how they can go further into a deeper form of forgiveness, then that is your memory and needs to be washed. If you see error in others, that's your creation. Secondly, if an adult is just beginning to heal childhood abuse or recent abuse, it may do them more harm than good to believe they created that experience, to take 100% responsibility for it. One step at a time. Ho'oponopono is an advanced forgiveness model and may not be for everyone. If Ho'oponopono makes someone feel worse, then they shouldn't practice it.

I have experimented with the H'oponopono prayer on the street with results that seemed miraculous. On three different occasions, two in the States and one in India, I was walking down the street and into situations where two or more people were having very heated arguments that appeared close to becoming physical fights. On each occasion I was off to the side and was not noticed by the participants. Common sense said I had nothing to do with those nasty scenes, to keep moving. Instead I dropped into Ho'oponopono mode: "Please forgive me for any time in this or past lives when I have become extremely belligerent in an argument and was threatening physical violence. I'm sorry for that. I love you. Thank you for the chance to heal these memories." I repeated those phrases for less than a minute and in each situation an amazing thing happened: the participants suddenly stopped arguing and either walked away or laughed and were instantly friendly again, as if a light bulb of reason and/or a wave of love had washed over them. As if the argument had never happened. As if what I had been witnessing was only a projected disturbing memory bubble of my own creation that was replaced by a more pleasant memory bubble of Divine creation.

Forgiveness at Layer 3 of the heart, the soul, is like a finger passing through air. We can't see it, yet there is some air turbulence created by the finger, the painful event, but resolution back to calm happens even faster than Layer 3.

> In God-realization the soul drops its separate consciousness and transcends duality in the abiding knowledge of its identity with the Infinite Reality. The shackles of limited individuality are broken; the world of shadows is at an end; the curtain of illusion is forever drawn. The feverishness and the agonizing distress of the pursuits of limited consciousness are replaced by the tranquility and bliss of Truth-consciousness. The restlessness and fury of temporal existence are swallowed up in the peace and stillness of Eternity. - Meher Baba[72]

LEVEL 4 OF THE HEART, the 'secret', *(sirr)* is the state of unity, of melting into the Ocean of Oneness like sugar dissolving in water. After we ask for forgiveness and return to a state of love and gratitude, we can allow the painful memories to simply vanish in the Ocean of divinity, where they no longer exist. The Ocean's wave washes away the footprints in the sand of our subconscious. Forgiveness becomes irrelevant because nothing ever happened.

Then the only moving finger is the finger of God, a traceless presence planting and nourishing the seeds of our Divinity as we sow and reap the long row that leads us home.

---

[69] *Discourses*, by Meher Baba, (6th Edition): Chapter, "The Nature of the Ego and Its Termination, Part i: The Ego As The Center of Conflict."

[70] Ibid: "*The New Humanity.*"

[71] Ibid: "*Maya.*"

[72] Ibid: "*The Formation and Function of Sanskaras.*"

Chapter Twenty-three
The Dance of Spirituality
and Psychology:
Forgiveness as a practice with Meher Baba

by Alisa Genovese
San Francisco, CA. Dec. 2016

THE DANCE OF SPIRITUALITY AND PSYCHOLOGY has informed all of my adult life. My relationship with psychology has been intertwined with my relationship to Meher Baba since the beginning.

I was born into a Roman Catholic family and had no exposure to Eastern philosophical thinking or psychology as a child. Although I felt a connection to Jesus, by high school I had declared myself agnostic, because none of the doctrine made sense to me. Deciding to go to college, I wanted to study psychology. I had never read a book on psychology; it was just a sudden flash of insight, which I mysteriously followed. In hindsight, I see it as the beginning of my awakening to seeking. I wanted to know and understand the deeper nature of reality so I thought, at that time, studying psychology was the way to achieve that understanding.

I started my study of psychology at Arizona State University in fall of 1979. In my sophomore year, I had taken a class in Eastern philosophy and mystical thinking, which set off a deep soul stirring that left me with a hunger to know more. I transferred to University of California Santa Barbara (UCSB) in my junior year in 1981. I was already becoming disheartened and dissatisfied with Western psychology. It wasn't offering me the answers I didn't even yet know I was seeking. While at UCSB I met Elias, the man who told me about Meher Baba.

Even before I heard about Meher Baba, I had started going to several workshops and seminars on campus about spirituality. I was particularly drawn to Eckankar, which promised soul travel and higher states of awakening, which were all very attractive to me by then. Elias was older than I was and clearly had a lot of spiritual experience and knowledge, to which I was increasingly drawn. I had never met anyone like him before. He had been a Baba lover for many years by then. He told me about Meher Baba just as I was ready to sign up to join Eckankar. As I was looking at the book *The Beloved*, he was telling me that Meher Baba was God in human form. I recall the first thing that came to me, as I looked at these amazing photographs of this beautiful man, was that Baba must be who He says He is because nobody could do what He did: say He was God in human form, keep silence for 40 years, and have nothing in His life disprove these assertions. I was nineteen years old.

I didn't know if Meher Baba was God, but I realized He was certainly not an ordinary human being. I felt a powerful familiarity with Him. When Elias told me that He dropped His body in 1969, I was disappointed; I felt I needed and wanted to have experiences of God. I wasn't interested in worshipping another Jesus on the cross. I found myself edging back to Eckankar, by now yearning for deeper experiences. Elias gave me the book

The Autobiography of a Yogi and recommended I read it if I was looking for a structured path. I felt a very strong draw to Paramahansa Yogananda. I became a devoted follower of Self-Realization Fellowship for 7 years, getting initiated into the highest form of meditation, which is called Kriya Yoga. Baba's photo was always with me on my altar as I meditated. I felt I was readying myself for Him. I feel now in hindsight that Baba led me to psychology and to Self-Realization Fellowship because I see now it was important for me to go inward to find Him before venturing outward.

By my senior year at UCSB, I was meditating twice a day, and I was growing more deeply connected to my spiritual life. I had finished all my requirements for my psychology major and I had nothing but electives left to take. Western psychology continued to lose interest for me as my focus was primarily shifted toward spiritual dimensions. I used my senior year to study religions exclusively, and I wound up getting a double BA in both Psychology and Religious Studies.

Within a year, I felt prompted to continue my studies in psychology. However, I now wanted something that could combine Western psychological thinking with Eastern philosophy. I didn't know if such a thing existed. In my search, I came upon Transpersonal Psychology, and it was exactly the synthesis of Eastern and Western philosophies I was looking for. I found the John F. Kennedy University in the Bay Area, which was co-founded by Allan Cohen, who I came to find out, was connected to Meher Baba. I knew immediately that was where I was going to go. It was the only school I applied to and I got in. I received a Master's Degree in Transpersonal Psychology in 1987.

For thirty years, I have pondered this interplay of the psychological and the spiritual: where and if they come together and where they diverge. Does psychological healing advance us spiritually? Is psychological healing necessary for spiritual growth? Does psychology play any part on the spiritual path? I have gradually come to believe that spiritual development is not dependent on psychological healing. Yet psychological healing can help us see what is underneath what we believe is real; driving the strangers from our hearts, strengthening our self-love, and enabling us the potential to surrender.

Baba says it so clearly here:

> The apparent is not real. Under many a life's complicated problems are hidden some of the simplest truths which the veil of ignorance obscures from human vision.

> So don't bother about believing in me. Be prepared to believe in your Self. [Have faith in your own capacity] for longing for Truth. Only then will you know Truth in its pure and infinite simplicity. Only then will you come to know who I am.[1]

Both my personal and professional work has always had this focus on the underlying opportunities available in psychological healing for spiritual growth. How do we get ourselves out of the way, trust ourselves enough to be able to hear the voice of intuition, the voice of Baba within? How to accomplish this most simple, yet perplexing task? From my psychological vantage point, getting out of the way has something to do with worthiness, worthiness to receive His Grace; the Grace of His Love, Guidance and Forgiveness. In my work over the years, with myself and other's suffering and pain, I have seen that movement toward ever-increasing self-love and self-acceptance is essential for deeper psychological healing and can subsequently benefit spiritual growth. I saw this truth so clearly in my own experience.

In my late twenties and thirties, I would travel to India yearly. On each journey I would always spend time sitting before Baba in the Samadhi. For many years when I would sit, I would internally hear Him ask, "Do you believe I love you?" Year after year the answer would be, "No!" I could not, did not, feel worthy of all He was giving me. This realization was very painful. Finally, after years of doing psychological healing, one day while sitting in the Samadhi, by now in my late thirties, when I heard Him ask me the same question, the answer that sprang spontaneously from within was, "Yes!" It was that clear and simple. Although He was with me all the time, finally there was enough self-love and worthiness to receive His Grace consciously, this Grace that He had been pouring on me continuously. What Baba was able to do through me grew immensely after this. I realized I was far more useful to Him in His work as a strong healthy person with a solid sense of worthiness. Here the psychological and the spiritual danced in joy!

I believe we are essentially powerless to completely heal ourselves. Our part, at best, is to soften and open to our worthiness, to allowing the Grace of Love to truly heal us.

How can you annihilate your own self? If you want to tear the veil, destroy your ego! How? All efforts to remove the veil strengthen it, and knots upon knots accumulate and become twisted tighter. The easiest way is to surrender your ego to me, regardless of how I handle it.[2]

Self-love becomes almost a prerequisite to receiving this Grace.

In this light I see the step of self-acceptance as essential on the spiritual path. We must own and face the ego, false or otherwise, before we can surrender it. There is no escape. There is no rising above. Those closest to Baba, His mandali, were the strongest, most loving, and self-possessed personalities I have ever encountered. Baba trained them in this way to be fearless. Whatever was beneath the surface was brought out, expressed, and then released, forgiven and forgotten. In the ashram with Baba, His Presence hastened this forgiveness theme. For us on the path, this self-acceptance and surrender is a gradual work in progress, probably over lifetimes.

After years of exploring the crossover between psychology and spirituality, I read *The Doorbell of Forgiveness* by Don Stevens with great curiosity. I had worked with forgiveness as a psychological step in healing with clients over the years, but I never connected it directly to Meher Baba or to a practice, or even as being a step on the spiritual path. This synthesis was interesting to me. Until I came across this work, I had never found any psychological healing work that can be used directly as a spiritual practice with Meher Baba.

The letting go through love is what Baba termed surrender. Is surrender possible without self-acceptance first? To me, surrender is not escape, or a rising above. It is a deeper commitment and love on all levels, to letting go and letting Him take over. What struck me in how forgiveness was being practiced and explored in the *The Doorbell of Forgiveness* was owning your part in whatever it is you are needing or wanting forgiveness for, and being able to face yourself so that you can actually have something to forgive and let go of, for yourself or toward the other. Suddenly, forgiveness became a path to deeper surrender, not just psychological healing. I could see the psychological healing of forgiveness as a tool to get closer to Baba, to surrendering to Him.

I attended my first of the two-day Forgiveness with Meher Baba Seminar hosted by Laurent in the Bay Area in March 2013. It was a powerfully inspiring weekend for me. I had never had that kind of intimate contact with my community. I knew many of the people who were sitting in that circle, for more than twenty years, and I had never seen that kind of openness and willingness to share. I saw their vulnerabilities, the things they were struggling with. It was a beautiful way to connect with my spiritual community. We all come together for Baba all the time, but it's difficult to allow ourselves to be that vulnerable. The forgiveness work gave everybody a stepping-stone on which to be vulnerable and it was moving and inspiring.

During the seminar, I volunteered to facilitate a breakout group. In that circle, participants continued to more deeply share their stories of what they were struggling with around forgiveness—with family members, co-workers, partners—and I was struck by how easy it seemed to be open with each other. It felt like Baba's magic: We were all there for Baba and focusing on forgiveness, and surrendering ourselves to Baba in that way, and suddenly it became easy to allow us to open to each other. I was witnessing people leaping off a cliff, trusting, exposing their vulnerabilities, and wanting to be able to forgive and let go.

I took this practice into my own life with Meher Baba. I went on to do two more seminars with Laurent, and then I facilitated a group in the Bay Area where we worked on practicing this forgiveness in our lives and sharing as a group. Through my own practice of forgiveness, I discovered I was doing self-acceptance work that He can directly help me with. And I experienced, so vividly, that He does help when I offered it to Him consciously in this way.

In the forgiveness journey, we are no doubt struggling with a psychological issue we must face fully. One has to go through the stages of the forgiveness cycle as laid out in this book. All these stages, however long they take, ready us for the letting go or surrendering it to Him. Using forgiveness as a spiritual practice will inevitably bring us face to face with our own self-acceptance and ultimately our need for our own self-forgiveness. Being able to forgive others is a measure, a degree, to which we can forgive ourselves. As we offer our dilemma before Baba, this offering becomes part of our surrender, part of our learning to rely on Him more and more fully. I believe this is where the psychological process crosses over into the spiritual. I now believe surrender is a core element in the journey of forgiving, especially forgiving with Meher Baba.

In my personal forgiveness practice, I began to see that it really takes me surrendering the whole problem I am struggling with to Baba before anything I am stuck with can really start to change, no matter how many efforts I have made. As long as my ego still wants to hold on to the problem in some way, I am going to struggle to be able to forgive. The ego will hold on tight to the ways it feels hurt, slighted, or shamed. So the surrendering process is about letting go of whatever it is you think is important, whatever you are holding on to. I think we get to the letting go or surrendering phase when we have had enough and we realize no matter how much anger, blame, or shame there is, nothing can be resolved until we are ready to let go into forgiveness. For me, that process is hastened or made more real by bringing it all before Meher Baba—all you have done; all you have experienced, felt, and processed, and yet still have not been able to forgive. This is the ripe moment of surrender. When we bring this part to Meher Baba, He takes over; He transforms it in ways our egos cannot fathom. From my understanding, this is the true spiritual journey with Him.

Ultimately, in surrender we are not asking Baba to take anything away, to make our lives better, but rather we are giving it to Him to do as He sees best for all involved. This is an important step in coming before Baba with your pain.

Seek me not to extricate you from your predicaments, but find me to surrender yourself wholeheartedly to my Will.... Do not ask me to bless you with a good job, but desire to serve me more diligently and honestly without expectation of reward. Never beg of me to save your life or the lives of your dear ones, but beg of me to accept you and permit you to lay down your life for me. Never expect me to cure you of your bodily afflictions, but beseech me to cure you of your ignorance. —Meher Baba[3]

There are many approaches one can take to letting go of your burden before Baba. In my own forgiveness journey, I sat before Baba with two very painful places of hurt and stuck wounding that had impacted my life dramatically. One concerned a friend and one concerned a family member. I had been struggling with both situations for some time. In my approach I chose to use a particular forgiveness prayer called the "H'oponopono Prayer," which is based on a Hawaiian forgiveness-healing model. It spoke to me because of its heartfelt simplicity; yet it has a powerful effect on ego holding. I found it very effective. I do not know much about the history of this cultural prayer nor have I learned how to use it within that tradition. None of that seemed to matter; I just brought it before Baba with my heart open and I laid bare my stuck places and asked Him take it and help me.

My practice was to take the name of the person I was struggling with and to say their name within the "H'oponopono Prayer," looking at Baba's image. For example:

"Lee, please forgive me, I am sorry, thank you for being my teacher, I love you."

I would say this prayer over and over before Baba until I could feel and meet my resistances and blocks, until my ego would cringe. At first I had to choke it out because the name of the person would create a reaction. However, by asking them to forgive me and thanking them for being my teacher, so much would flush to the surface to be left before Baba. I felt He was there with so much compassion; I could begin to let go, more and more. I could feel my hurt and anger in a safer way, without all the pain and self-judgment. With practice, I could begin to see my part of it without shame or suppression. It grew softer, more accepting. The healing of the Divine began to surface as a small voice within my heart and I could hear it. I could trust it; I could finally begin to let go the grip of the pain and anger.

That was my part. From there Baba's magic unfolded in a most natural and organic way. Everything that felt so immovable before began to soften and shift. In my case, regarding my male friend, it truly did feel like magic. I'd been long struggling to forgive him because of his vicious verbal attacks on me, which had not only deeply wounded me, but also had dramatically impacted my life. We were part of a close knit community that meet together regularly, and the toxicity of his attack affected not only the community as a whole, but in particular and most dramatically my relationship with his girlfriend, who was both my housemate and very close friend. So this attack went deep and affected many. As much as I had processed it within myself and with so many others, including him, I could not get past it, I could not forgive him. It actually grew worse for a long time. It was at this point I took it to Baba. To repeat the prayer that I forgave him and thanked him for being my teacher was very difficult when I was so hurt by his actions. It really brought me up against my own ego and pride, as well as all the places I was shutting the door to my own heart. "Thank you for being my teacher." This sentence was probably the most powerful part of this practice for me. As I would say "thank you for being my teacher," I couldn't take it; there was resistance to opening to that feeling of gratitude for his presence in my life when I still had so much anger. I had to really work to turn the whole mess over to Baba because I was powerless to make the situation better or to bring healing to it. I just had to let go enough to allow Baba to do it. My only work was letting go. That was the most forgiving thing I could do.

Eventually with practice, I started to feel and hear something Kabir spoke of: being grateful for those who hurt you or harm you, they take your sanskaras (impressions) from you. I started to feel something new arise, something I could apply to my situation. When I would say, "Thank you for being my teacher," it started to mean, "thank you for coming into my life and giving me the opportunity to look at myself, to come up against the places that my heart is closed, where you become other and I can't let you in; all of these gifts that you bring me in what you did." This new opening was the gift He gave me when I listened.

The beauty of this practice is that the other person does not have to know you are doing this work. It is not about condoning their behavior or having to resolve the problem. Forgiveness with Meher Baba, at its core, is an energetic psycho-spiritual practice. None of the people that I experienced movement or healing with ever knew I was doing this work, nor did I ever share it with them. It was between Baba and I. It doesn't really matter if I ever process this situation again with this person, or if I ever come to some understanding: it is the energy that shifts in my own heart. Suddenly, I started to feel differently about them, I started to feel differently about the whole problem; the grip that it had on me began to loosen. In the process, my heart was freed. Once the heart is freed, the mind can follow.

In my case, I found nothing short of magic occurred as I practiced this forgiveness work before Baba. Years of stuck energy began to move most naturally. For example, after practicing for some weeks around the man who so hurt me, I ran into him in a store after not seeing him for some time, and it took some charge off. He then invited me to his birthday party. Previously, I could not even tolerate seeing him; I was so trapped by the anger. We tried to process it, and it only made it worse. I had reached a place where I felt I never wanted to talk to him again. So when he invited me to his party and I felt a natural "yes" arise, I was surprised. I could feel Baba's hand involved. Even more beautiful was that when I arrived at his party, he greeted me so warmly and really made an effort to be loving and kind towards me. He even apologized and took some ownership for what had happened. He had never behaved that way toward me since the incident. I have nothing else to offer as a reason than this letting go and letting Baba. We are not friends now, nor is he in my life, but the charge is gone. I feel warmth in my heart for all I learned from him. Even as I still do not condone what he did, none of that matters anymore, because it is not in my heart any longer.

This is just one example of how this forgiveness practice worked in my life. I have had several profound experiences where energy completely shifted. These experiences really made me believe that forgiveness is possible. We can forgive, we can shift this energy; it all comes down to willingness to surrender it and to really allow Baba to come in and help with it.

After years of being a Transpersonal therapist and exploring the connection between the psychological and spiritual realms, where they meet and where they depart, this practice offered me a new view. I've always imagined the psychological as presenting an opportunity for spiritual growth, but to see and experience using a psychological process of a hurt or slight as a direct spiritual practice with Meher Baba is where I found power and beauty in this work. It offers a guide to practice surrendering to Him.

At the time of this writing, I was deeply touched to learn of the forgiveness ceremony that united Natives and veterans at Standing Rock, ND. This came after the victory to halt further construction on the Dakota Access Pipeline through sacred native land. I had been closely been following the horrors that developed as the "Water Protectors" stood their ground against the forces of greed and ignorance, and remained strong through the hard won battle. So to hear of this forgiveness ceremony, as I wrote this chapter, was a beautiful reminder of the power of forgiveness.

This ceremony was forgiveness in a most courageous form. To see the "White Man" bow before the native elders, and ask for forgiveness for the historical wrongs and harms done to their people, was a rare sight, and certainly a step toward the reparations needed. That kind of forgiveness takes courage and true heart, and yet is a necessary step to release the pain held by both sides. It was indeed a symbolic gesture forgiving centuries of oppression, opening the way toward healing and uniting.

And as Chief Leonard Crow Dog, an elder of the Lakota Nation so aptly said, speaking of world peace, "We do not own the land, the land owns us." To witness this gave me such hope – to see that it is never too late to ask for forgiveness. It is never too late to heal the deeply held wounds of arrogance, domination and disrespect.

Jai Baba

––––––––––––––––

1. ~Lord Meher, 1937, pg. 1883, online version
2. ~Lord Meher, 1960, pg. 4676 online version
3. ~Meher Baba Divya Vani, vol. 1 no 8 (1960) pg. 42

Chapter Twenty-Four
Impermanence, Expectations, and Gratitude

by Chickie Jacobs
January 2017

> "The root of suffering is attachment"
> - Lord Buddha

I HAVE LONG BEEN INTERESTED IN THE SUBJECT OF FORGIVENESS, both from a personal perspective of how to navigate life, and simply in the curiosity of human behavior. Once you begin any earnest search for an understanding of what defines forgiveness, the theoretical ideas come pretty fast and furious; not unlike the events in our lives that force us to confront forgiveness in the first place. I acknowledge that forgiveness is an essential part of any measure of growth and spirituality. I also acknowledge it is one of the most important parts of a relationship. Carrying around unforgiven resentment, anger, hatred, or blame toward others is both unproductive and unhealthy. I may even think I know what forgiveness looks like, from both the giver and receiver's perspective. I have often said – I think once forgiveness has occurred, both parties no longer feel like the forgiven issue (or event) is any of their business. It no longer elicits significant feelings within either of them. Perhaps that it just what it feels like to me?

The many approaches to forgiveness are as varied as the things that require forgiveness. And so, no single approach is going to fit all situations.

However there is at least a theoretical connection between gratitude and forgiveness, which has an almost universal application. I propose that is because of the role which expectations play in almost every instance where a person feels hurt and forgiveness seems necessary.

There are many people who believe that forgiveness is a process which ends with (or at least includes), some form of contrition and a type of restoration (or reconciliation). Many times, this is both possible and ideal. However, there are also certain instances where contrition is not forthcoming and restoration is also impossible. In such cases, forgiveness remains possible, but it is not necessarily a process in which both forgiver and forgiven negotiate together. Rather, an understanding is achieved by the forgiver – through detachment from any notions of permanence, which have created a framework under which expectations have led to disappointment and pain.

Notions of permanence which set up such expectations breed two major conflicts. The first is the idea regarding the way things should be, according to needs, desires, and embraced perspectives about morality and social contracts. The second is the belief that the way things should be is only meaningful if it is consistent and therefore permanent.

Says who?

Nothing in life, including life itself, is permanent.

In nature, things begin – live – and then end without any fanfare, in a pattern which, in and of itself, normalizes and even celebrates impermanence.

Likewise, impermanence in human experience does not automatically have to have a negative connotation. When things are the way I think they should be, it pleases me and naturally, I want them to remain this way permanently. However, by the very nature of life, there is really no such thing as permanence and people cannot constantly or permanently meet my expectations (or preconceived notions) about the way things should be. This is because – the way things should be – is different for each and every person. There is no universal set of absolutes when it comes to the way things should be. So, when our expectations are met, that is more often (and more likely) to be an exception rather than the rule.

INDIVIDUALLY UNIQUE NEEDS:

As an example, my close friends and I share many similar ideas and values. It is safe to say that our notions of morality are pretty well aligned with one another. However, even in our relatively small and homogenous group, there are many and varied points of departure when it comes to what constitutes "good" or "bad" behavior. Also, what upsets or injures one person does not necessarily translate to the other members of the group. In the same way, what pleases one may not please another. And this is because things that hurt or heal each of us, are based almost entirely on our individually unique needs, desires, fears, and expectations.

While there may be some things we can all agree upon, there will be some that we simply do not. And although all people have the right to feel hurt, betrayed, or rejected (or any number of other strong emotions) about the behaviors of others, the only thing I have the power to control is my own perceptions and reactions.

I do not have the right to determine for another person the way things should be. And when I cease to issue demands on others about this, I simultaneously regain some measure of control over our my own contentment, and release all others from the almost inescapable position of disappointing me.

This is more than compassion. This is actually my acceptance of the reality that humans will act in a way that they believe will reduce their own suffering, and increase their own pleasure – and sometimes those actions are in direct conflict with the expectations I have set up.

Many times in relationships, the need for forgiveness comes out of an assumption of permanence. Not just that the relationship itself will be permanent, but that the positive feelings, and sense of connection we experience with a person, will consistently and permanently fulfill our expectations.

However, in my experience such expectations do not line up neatly when humans are involved. People have conflicting needs. People have their own ideas about what love is. People grow and change. People carry around demons from the past (I sure do). People hurt people, sometimes out of selfishness or cruelty, and sometimes simply out of expressing themselves naturally and spontaneously.

And so, when I feel hurt by the actions of people I love (the people who I expect to love me in return), and especially when the relationship is irrevocably damaged by such actions, I feel injured and seek contrition and restoration. But, what if I was hurt less by the actions themselves than by – my perception of the transience of something I originally believed would be permanent?

I met a man in 1995 who ended up being the love of my life. However, for a variety of reasons, we could not sustain the relationship. Even though we tried to keep it alive, on and off, for nearly 20 years, we could not.   Many promises were broken, many harsh words spoken, and the trust evaporated. But there were moments of being so intoxicated by the perfection of our shared experience that I almost felt as if God had specifically made us for each other. And perhaps that was true. But God's hand in it wasn't enough for permanence, and the relationship ended anyway. Sometimes, love isn't enough.

As much as I feel that loss every day, I know that many people have had the same experience of not ending up with "the love of their lives." Probably just as many people have never experienced that kind of love at all. For those who have loved and lost, it is common to want to avoid the memories of those shared moments (or even to feel as if it was wasted time because it eventually ended). This is a form of resentment, and a sign that forgiveness has not yet taken place.

For a large part of my adult life, I have had the blessing of that strong, profound connection to someone. It ended anyway. And as much as I acknowledge the impossibility of that relationship continuing on the trajectory that I thought it would, I equally acknowledge that there were moments when I felt perfectly loved, perfectly connected, and perfectly content. So, why would I avoid those memories? Why would I view those experiences as wasted time? Because it hurts. Because of the fact that those experiences were not a constant and permanent part of the rest of my life – ad infinitum. It felt to me both unfair and injurious.

Those questions just made me reflect on the inevitable impermanence of everything, not just as a way to reduce the suffering I continue to feel over the loss of this relationship, but also as a way to examine the parameters for which forgiveness seems necessary at all. Delving into it made me want to go forward with gratitude that I ever experienced that kind of love, rather than believing that the only way it matters is if it is mine forever after.

The saying, "gratitude is the opposite of anger," is not a new idea. It gets relegated to the heaping pile of platitudes that look great on bumper stickers, or Facebook, but are significantly harder to practice while enduring intense personal pain. When it comes to forgiving people I have deeply loved, and who have hurt me especially, i. It's been difficult for me to feel grateful for the experiences of love that I've had in my life without also being aware of (and assigning blame for) the reasons why those experiences are no longer a present.

I have found that with many of the people I know (including myself), we habitually attach the relationship, and all of its memories and experiences, to its ultimate terminus. Have you ever been deeply in love? Are you still together? Why not?

By answering such questions, we are ultimately brought to a place of assigning blame, or defining events, which led to the relationship's end. Rarely do either of these actions lead to more gratitude, because of the focus on negative results, rather than the individual experiences gained.

This also does not address our expectations and whether or not they're reasonable; not just reasonable for us to ask in general but reasonable for the situation in which we are asking for them.

For me to ask one person to do something may be well received and granted without question. And I may be even glad to offer the things I am asking for in return. But, that does not mean that the things I am asking for will be well received by everyone else. In fact, the thing I am asking for may, in fact, be impossible for some people to deliver. So, I have to cater my expectations carefully to the person and situation at hand, further proof for me that there is no universal way to determine – the way things should be.

When I believe that someone has purposefully denied me something that I feel I need, and especially if the thing I need was something I believed was a shared priority, it makes blame and avoidance come much easier -- and forgiveness and gratitude are much harder for me. This is especially true when I assume that forgiveness requires an act of restoration. Because, in the case of trying to forgive someone who I wanted to spend the rest of my life with – and I believe that their behavior (or choices) thwarted that from happening, then the only actual, acceptable restoration is for the relationship to pick up where it left off (better than ever, of course), and continue permanently.

But, if that relationship cannot be restored, and if in the end, I cannot continue on that expected trajectory with the person I love, I have a hard time finding value in the experiences we shared. I have an even harder time forgiving the wrongs which I perceived were the cause of this relationship's ruin.

Valuing something for however long it is mine to experience is perhaps the greatest expression of gratitude I can have, and it sets up far fewer instances when my expectations cannot be met. Detaching my ideas of happiness from the impossible expectation of permanence allows me to not only value experiences in real time, but also to continue valuing them even after they have ended.

If I take a trip somewhere, I know it is not going to last forever. I acknowledge that it is a temporary timeframe and a temporary locale. I am able to value and honor the memories made on that trip, and I continue to look on it fondly, even though it is temporary. Even if it is the best time of my life; the most fun, fulfilling experience I've ever had, I do not decrease the value of the adventure simply because it did not last forever. I go into that adventure with unconditional awareness and acceptance of its impermanence. In fact, the thing that makes it so special and significant is that it provides me with experiences and memories that stand out.

Why not start approaching relationships like this: being grateful for the "standout" experiences instead of postulating that the only way they are valuable and meaningful is if they continue to provide fun, fulfillment, and happiness forever? This may allow me to find myself having fewer expectations, and being less hurt when my expectations aren't met (or when relationships change and sometimes even dematerialize, as can easily happen over the course of a normal human lifetime).

In the case of the man I met in 1995, I want to be able to think about our most special memories together without becoming despondent, angry, and hopeless. I believe that I need to forgive him. I was hurt by his actions which led to our relationship's demise. I actually had a long list of grievances and specific events or actions which I could easily point to – This and that is to blame.

However, once I start to reflect on impermanence and gratitude, I realize three things:

• I defined his actions as horrible based on my interpretation of the way things should be.
• Rarely did his actions occur without some reaction from me that only made things worse.
• The real cause of my enduring pain was that the relationship (and its positive elements) were neither consistent nor permanent.

Two people can love each other deeply, connect on a profound level, and believe that they will be together forever, maybe even based on promises or plans made together. But, those agreements about an ambiguous future are made in an unambiguous present moment – usually in moments when the connection is the strongest – and, as much as those promises or plans may be genuine in those present moments, they are not a permanent obligation. Because nothing is permanent.

It was so meaningful to me when we were connecting in a loving way, that in moments when we failed to achieve that (or could no longer do so), it felt like a theft; something to be angry about; something to find blame for; something that would require my forgiveness.

Without my expectations of how things should be, I was led to the awareness that most of his supposed "crimes" were directly related to my expectations of permanence. I wanted that love, those feelings, and those experiences to be a perpetual part of my life. When I realized that they wouldn't be, I felt that something had been stolen from me. All that was stolen from me was my own expectations. I felt hurt when the inevitable impermanence of everything was revealed.

Must two people end up together forever, and must their profound connection be a constant in order for those beautiful moments to have meaning?

No.

They will continue to have value on their own, as long as I detach them from my expectations. Those memories, just like memories of a wonderful journey somewhere, can and should have value simply because they existed at all. And that's where my gratitude comes in.

Gratitude allows me to forgive the actions of another and to see those behaviors as an expressions of their needs and desires – as opposed to crimes against me personally. We all have a role to play in the construction of our own expectations.

In my case, my assumptions of permanence diminished the magical experiences, both in the moments of conflict and after the relationship finally ended, simply because things weren't the way I thought they should be. I realize now, that it was the moments in which I had zero expectations at all which corresponded with the moments of deepest connection between us.

Detaching from the assumption of permanence, then, is not only a great way to avoid much of the hurt which I experience in any given moment, but it is also a way to forgive those who have inevitably hurt me by not meeting my expectations. Ultimately, I must acknowledge that the notion of permanence does not allow other people to articulate themselves in a natural or spontaneous way. This is because it demands unconditional uniformity of both expression and experience to me, and that is not really possible. My idea that romantic love must feel good every moment and also has to last forever, is both unworkable and unreasonable. Who could live up to this expectation, ever?

If instead I approach people and experiences as having value in the present moment, and I also detach from any notions of permanence (mandating another's actions), I am at once reducing my own suffering, and allowing myself to feel gratitude for moments that happen to meet my needs and please me. This paves the way for true forgiveness.

In fact, I may even realize that there is nothing to forgive.

The quote from Lord Buddha is in: "The Middle Length Discourses of the Buddha", 2nd Edition, (Somerville, MA: Wisdom Publications, 1995), by Bhikkhu Bodhi, p.868

Chapter Twenty-Five
End of the Spear

By Tracey Schmidt

Roll the stone away from the tomb where your heart has lain:
It has become an incubating grief which, at your own hand
has become a weapon.

Running from yourself at all costs –
discovering too late that you have become
A tourist instead of a pilgrim -
Or loud instead of powerful…

Given up for dead
but only sleeping,
coax yourself awake again by
whispering into your sure and eventual release.

The thorn, lodged into that once tender spot,
has fallen out from the sound of your own voice.
That which flowers from the vine wants to
remind you that
this beauty
was always meant for you.

Nothing lightens the weight of the world
like laying our burdens down
and dropping the spear
we point against ourselves.

Consider becoming your own wild and faithful companion.
Turn out the light you have left on
night after sleepless night because of fear –

And, seeing the star veil hatch a firmament
Listen -
They are whispering their love language, saying:
Forgive yourself.

About the Contributing Authors

About Meher Baba, by Sarah Weichberger
Flagstaff, Arizona (April 2016)

MERWAN S. IRANI WAS BORN to Persian Zoroastrian parents in Pune India in 1894. His parents were both Iranian and settled in India. He experienced spiritual enlightenment as a young man during his college days, through an encounter with Hazrat Babajan, the great Sufi master. He became known as a spiritual master, and his early disciples named him Meher Baba which means compassionate one. He proclaimed himself "The Avatar of the Age," and he moved to an abandoned British military camp near the remote village of Arangaon where he lived with his twelve Mandali (disciples). This initial residence is called Meherabad. He also built a residence called Meherazad where he lived until his death in 1969. Baba has many followers from all over the world as well as Indian devotees. For his spiritual work, he chose to remain silent at the age of 31, in 1925, and he remained silent until his death. He spent his life in service, helping those in need. He was especially focused on helping lepers and also masts, who are individuals that are "God intoxicated" and therefore have trouble functioning on the earthly plane.

Meher Baba first came to the United States in 1931, and with the help of his western followers, he built a universal spiritual retreat center in Myrtle Beach, South Carolina. This Center served as his "Home in the West," and it is still an active retreat center where his followers from all over the world can visit and commune with Baba. There are many documentary films that have been made about Baba and his life, and the Baba center has an extensive library that includes these films as well as numerous writings by Baba and his Mandali. There are also many volumes of spiritual writings from all faiths.

Don Stevens was one of Meher Baba's early Western followers and he became one of Baba's inner circle. Don met Baba in 1952, in New York City. Meher Baba considered Don one of his Mandali, even though he wasn't living in India. Don spent most of his life after meeting Baba working on writing projects given to him by Baba, and after Baba's passing in 1969, chronicling his own experiences with Baba. Don passed away in 2011, at the age of 92, and was working on a book at that time titled *Three Snapshots of Reality* which was published shortly after he passed away in London.

ASPEN WEICHBERGER is a recent graduate from Embry-Riddle University. She currently lives and works in Arizona but enjoys traveling. She has a varied spiritual life but holds a deep love and respect for Meher Baba. Aspen is still working on her own forgiveness path, but collaboration on this book has helped her immensely.

DR. ALISTAIR COCKBURN, part engineer and part poet, has been a cultural bridge most of his life. Of English parents, raised mostly in the U.S., he lived in Sri Lanka and Bangladesh in his early youth, Scotland and Sweden as a teenager, and Switzerland, Norway, France and Argentina as an adult. The essay in this book represents his first non-technical and non-poetry writing. Much of his writing can be seen at http://alistair.cockburn.us. His favorite activities are dancing, sitting underwater, and sleeping.

JOE DISABATINO, M.ED. worked for twenty years as a psychotherapist with a specialty in family therapy, a workshop leader/ trainer, business coach and leadership development trainer. He has studied Sufi Healing and other forms of transpersonal healing and coaching. He has lived and worked abroad, including England for eight years and India for over four years. Joe is also an artist--he has a passion for painting, writing and directing plays, and poetry. He resides in Myrtle Beach, SC where he conducts workshops and seminars on a variety of personal growth topics, leads meditation classes, paints, and does volunteer work.

ALISA GENOVESE was Born and raised in New York. At 19 years of age, she had the great good fortune to hear Meher Baba's name in her junior year of college. Her life has been guided by Him since, including spending 7 years on a meditation path with Paramahansa Yogananda before going to India the first time in 1986 to meet Meher Baba's Mandali. She has traveled to India twenty times since then spending many wonderful weeks with the Mandali and learning what it meant to surrender one's life to Him. She was married to Robert Dreyfuss and together they raised two beautiful children. She is a private practice psychotherapist for over twenty-eight years and has worked extensively with individuals and groups.

RANDALL OVERDORFF has practiced psychotherapy in Gainesville Georgia for thirty years. He is credentialed as a counselor, marriage and family therapist, EMDR therapist and art therapist. For twelve years he specialized in the treatment of traumatized children. He is interested in learning and helping others to embody love in action in daily life.

TRACEY SCHMIDT is an internationally recognized poet and photographer. Her first book of poetry, *I Have Fallen in Love with the World,* (Turtle Dove Publications, 2015) has garnered rave reviews. Much of poetry has been reprinted in anthologies, poetry journals and blogs worldwide. She teaches creativity and poetry all over the country.   More of her work can be seen at: www.traceyschmidt.com. She lives in Asheville, NC with her two hives of bees, a cat and a turtle dove. She has fallen in love with the world. She is still not sure how it happened.

JENNIFER TINSMAN is a retired life coach and former owner of Quantum Track Life Coaching, LLC. She has been a follower of the teachings of Meher Baba since 1971.

VANESSA WEICHBERGER is an artist and teacher. She has been a follower of Meher Baba since 1972. While she has no formal credentials she has more life experience than can possibly be explained in a short blurb about herself.

CHICKIE JACOBS is an amateur writer, musician, artist, carpenter, and philosopher who contributes to the online forum, "Forgiveness with Meher Baba." She is the proud mother of Angela who is senior at Western Washington University, and lives in the foothills of the Cascade Mountains with her two dogs, Doodle and BooBoo.

LAURENT WEICHBERGER has been involved with Meher Baba since 1986. Since then he has striven to balance his mind and heart, by actively engaging in the world as a computer software developer and teacher, while not being of it. Along the way he met Don E. Stevens, and they worked together from 2002 until Don's death in 2011. Laurent teaches "Big Data" for an international software company, and facilitates seminars on Forgiveness with Meher Baba when he is invited to do so.

AMRIT IRANI : In January 1968 Baba's younger brother Adi Jr. discussed with Baba at Meherazad a plan to marry his son Dara to a young woman named Amrit (age 18), who was the daughter of Baba's disciple Kumar. This match had been suggested by Baba's beloved Mehera. On December 23, 1968 they were married and Baba blessed their union at Meherazad. This would be the last marriage Baba would personally bless. Amrit has spent her entire life dedicated to her lord Avatar Meher Baba, and faithfully serves him at Meherabad, as part of the committee which is in charge of Meherabad Hill, and beloved Baba's Samadhi. She travels around the world speaking about Meher Baba and sharing stories of life with Him.

SHU-YI HSU is an educator, instructional designer, and researcher. She is pursuing her doctoral studies at Columbia University. Shu-Yi started her spiritual journey and attended her first forgiveness workshop in 2017. She also goes to church on Sundays and enjoys a spiritual and mindfulness discussion. Shu-Yi currently resides in New York and is developing her career in online education.

Acknowledgements

AVATAR MEHER BABA, for being and loving, and guiding my path back to Him, step by blessed step.

DON E. STEVENS, my Beautiful Big Bear for mentoring me, and showing me love and tenderness on the path back to our Father, Meher Baba.

DANIEL J. SANDERS, for the finest toothed comb in editing history, backed by deepening wisdom.

ALISTAIR, ALISA, ASPEN, RANDY, JOE, AND JENNIFER, all you have contributed to this book has made it more wondrous, thank you.

AMRIT AND SHU-YI, while coming late to this forgiveness party you certainly showed up in a glorious fashion with all you shared, thank you.

ALISON GOVI HUTTER many thanksfor her extraordinary graphic representation of the Forgiveness Life-Cycle diagram, it is lovely.

TRACEY SCHMIDT, for your wondrous poem which resurrects the spiritual meaning of the word forgiveness.

VANESSA, for loving me, and all you have contributed to this book, fabulous! Mi corazon.

EDMOND LEGUM, for a last minute cover layout and design which is the talk of the town. Great work!

KARL MOELLER, for his supercalifragilistic work on the layout and design of this book, you rock!

Suggested Further Reading

MEHER BABA RELATED PUBLICATIONS:

A Mirage Will Never Quench Your Thirst: A Source of Wisdom about Drugs, Compiled and edited by Laurent Weichberger & Laura Smith
(Myrtle Beach: Sheriar Foundation, 2003) - 141p.
http://www.amazon.com/Mirage-Will-Never-Quench-Thirst/dp/188061927X/

Related article: *Ayahuasca This Way Comes*, by Laurent Weichberger (Flagstaff: The Noise, 2008): on-line at http://issuu.com/ompoint/docs/ayahuascathiswaycomes

Meher Baba's Word and His Three Bridges, by Don E. Stevens with Norah Moore, and Laurent Weichberger (London: Companion Books, 2003) - 234p.
http://www.amazon.com/Meher-Babas-Word-Three-Bridges/dp/0952509741/

Meher Baba's Gift of Intuition, by Don E. Stevens and Companions (London: Companion Books, 2006). - 197p.
http://www.amazon.com/Meher-Babas-Intuition-Stevens-Companions/dp/0952509768/

Celebrating Divine Presence: Journeys into God, by Laurent Weichberger, Yaakov Weintraub, Karl Moeller, et al (London: Companion Books, 2008) - 392p.
http://www.amazon.com/Celebrating-Divine-Presence-Journeys-into/dp/0952509792/

The Doorbell of Forgiveness, by Don E. Stevens with his Young People's Group (London: Companion Books, 2011). - 290p.
http://www.amazon.com/Doorbell-Forgiveness-Don-E-Stevens/dp/095250975X

Three Snapshots of Reality, by Don E. Stevens with Wayne Smith (London: Companion Books, 2014). - 133p.
http://www.amazon.com/Three-Snapshots-Reality-Don-Stevens/dp/0956553001/

Discourses, by Meher Baba, Revised 6th Edition (Myrtle Beach: Sheriar Foundation, 2007) ~ 904p.
http://www.sheriarbooks.org

God Speaks, by Meher Baba (2nd edition, 1973. Fourth Printing), ~ 313p. http://www.sheriarbooks.org

CONFLICT RESOLUTION AND PSYCHOLOGY:

Home Coming, Reclaiming and Healing your Inner Child, by John Bradshaw (New York: Bantam, 1990).

The Anatomy of Peace, Resolving the Heart of Conflict, by The Abringer Institute (San Francisco: Berrett-Koehler, 2008).

A Little Book on the Human Shadow, by Robert Bly (New York: Harper One, 1988).

Owning Your Own Shadow, Understanding the Dark Side of the Psyche, by Robert A. Johnson (New York: Harper One, 1991).